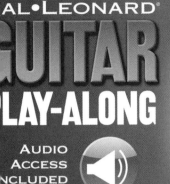

HAL•LEONARD®

GUITAR PLAY-ALONG

AUDIO ACCESS INCLUDED

PLAYBACK+
...eed • Pitch • Balance • Loop

GRATEFUL DEAD

VOL. 186

T0066243

CONTENTS

To access audio visit:
www.halleonard.com/mylibrary

Enter Code
2350-0958-9565-9550

Cover photo © Retna

ISBN 978-1-4950-0696-8

HAL•LEONARD®
CORPORATION
7777 W. BLUEMOUND RD. P.O. BOX 13819 MILWAUKEE, WI 53213

For all works contained herein:
Unauthorized copying, arranging, adapting, recording, Internet posting, public performance,
or other distribution of the printed or recorded music in this publication is an infringement of copyright.
Infringers are liable under the law.

Visit Hal Leonard Online at
www.halleonard.com

Casey Jones

Words by Robert Hunter
Music by Jerry Garcia

Intro
Moderately ♩ = 99

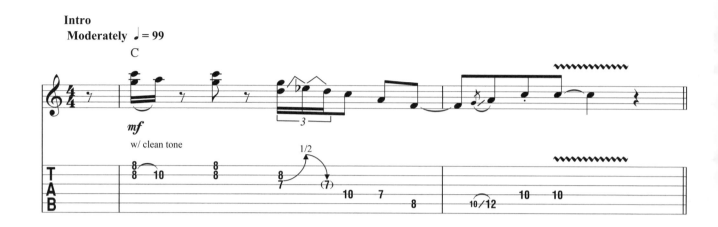

Chorus

Driv - in' that train, ___ high on co - caine. ___ Cas - ey Jones, you'd bet - ter

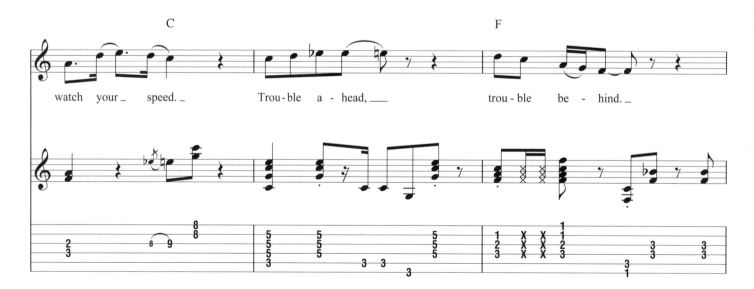

watch your ___ speed. ___ Trou - ble a - head, ___ trou - ble be - hind. ___

Copyright © 1970 ICE NINE PUBLISHING CO., INC.
Copyright Renewed
All Rights Administered by UNIVERSAL MUSIC CORP.
All Rights Reserved   Used by Permission

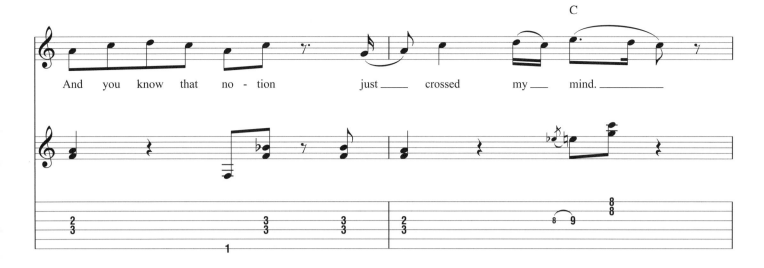

And you know that no - tion just ___ crossed my ___ mind. ___

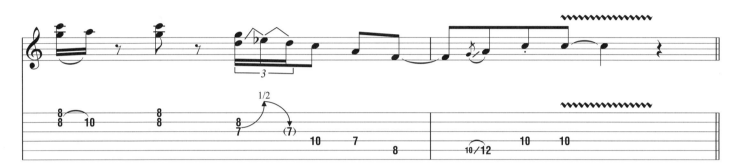

Verse

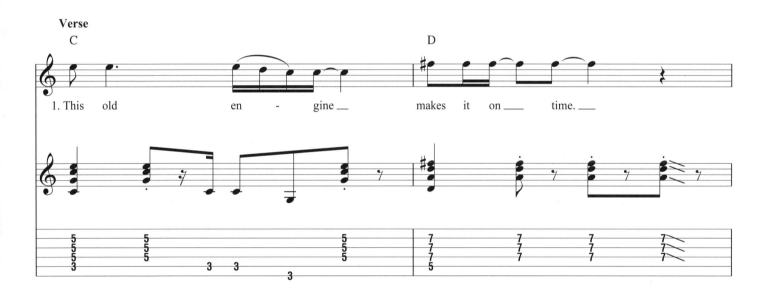

1. This old en - gine ___ makes it on ___ time. ___

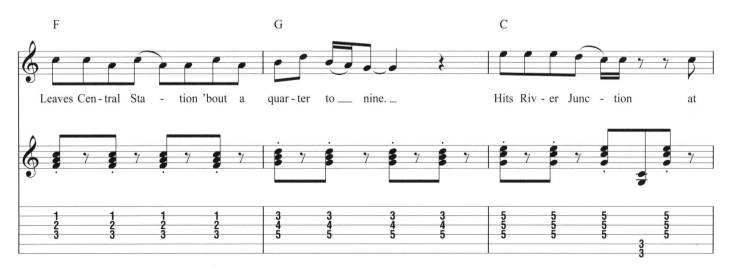

Leaves Cen - tral Sta - tion 'bout a quar - ter to ___ nine. ___ Hits Riv - er Junc - tion at

Verse

2. Trou-ble a-head, a _____ la-dy in red. _____ Take my ad - vice _____ you'd __ be

*Bass plays A.

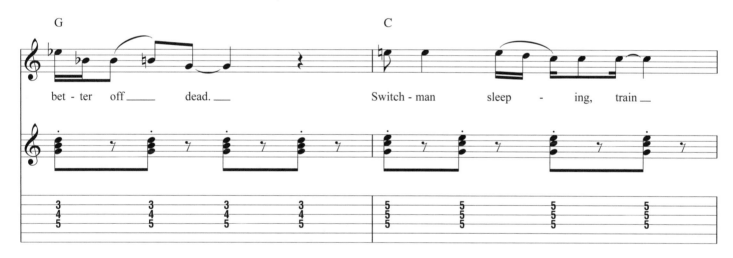

bet - ter off _____ dead. _____ Switch - man sleep - ing, train _____

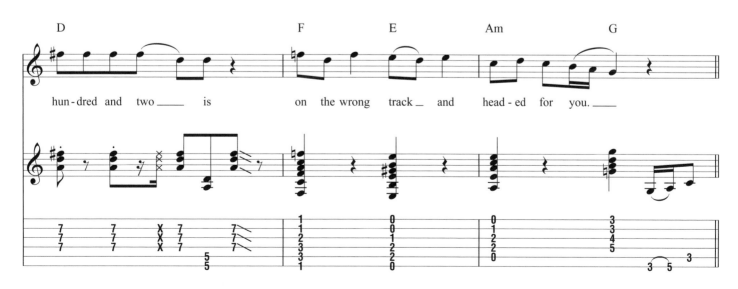

hun-dred and two _____ is on the wrong track __ and head-ed for you. _____

Chorus

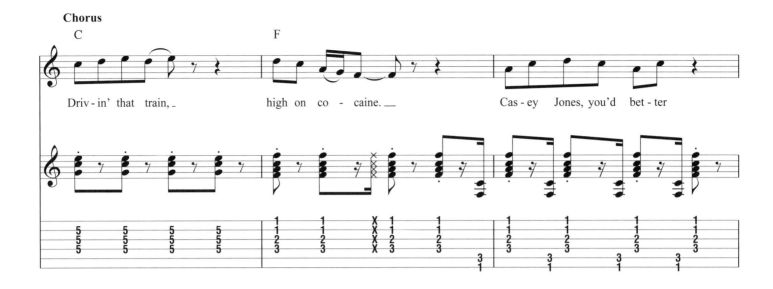

Driv-in' that train, high on co-caine. Cas-ey Jones, you'd bet-ter

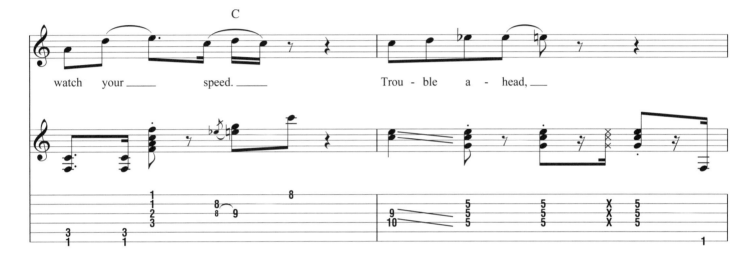

watch your speed. Trou-ble a-head,

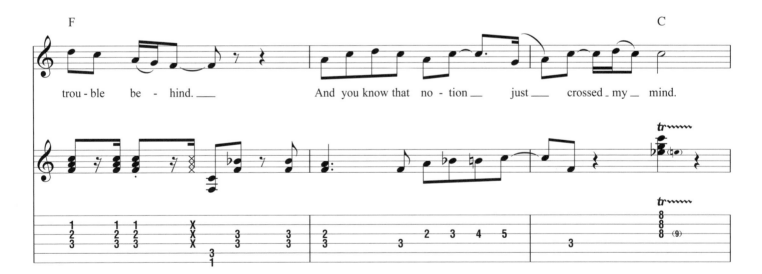

trou-ble be-hind. And you know that no-tion just crossed my mind.

Interlude

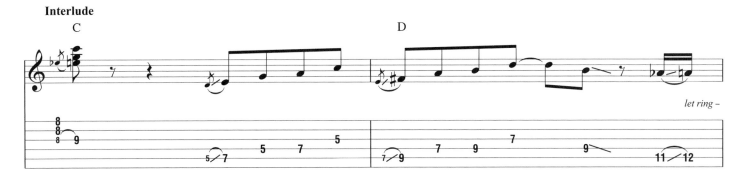

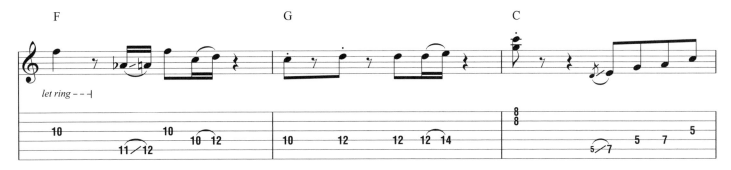

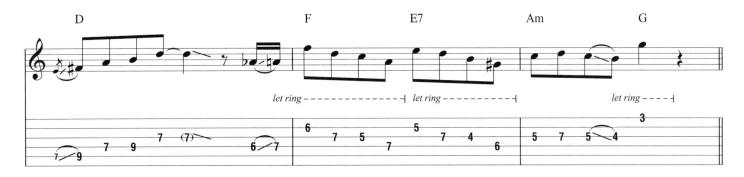

Guitar Solo

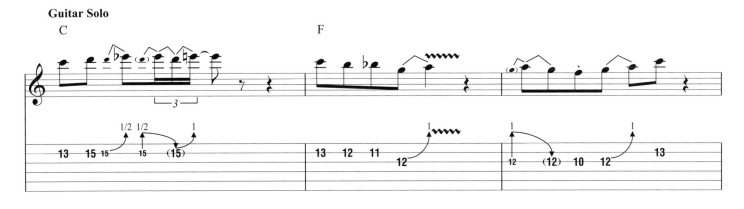

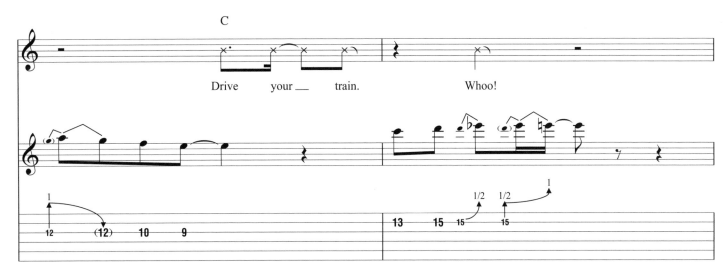

Drive your __ train.   Whoo!

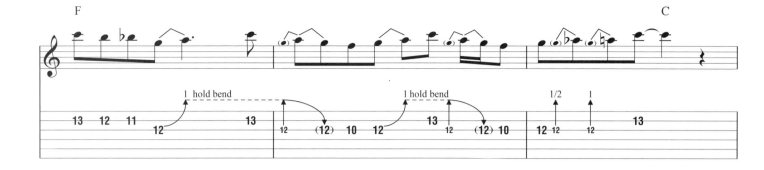

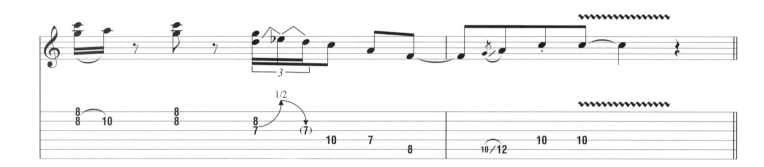

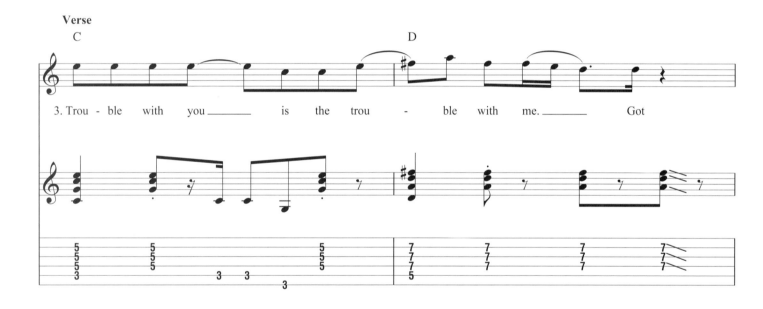

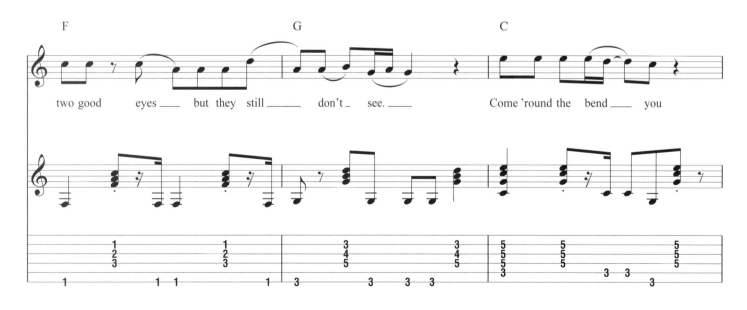

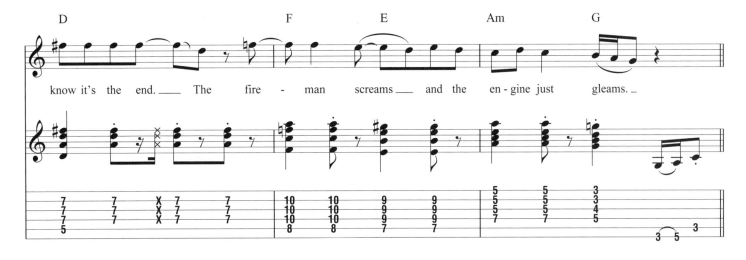

know it's the end.___ The fire - man screams___ and the en - gine just gleams.___

Outro-Chorus

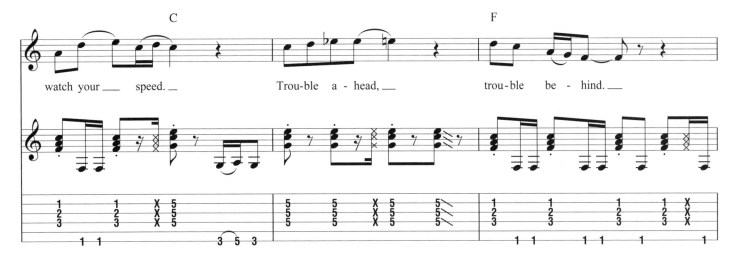

Driv-ing that train,___ high on co - caine.___ Cas - ey Jones, you'd bet - ter

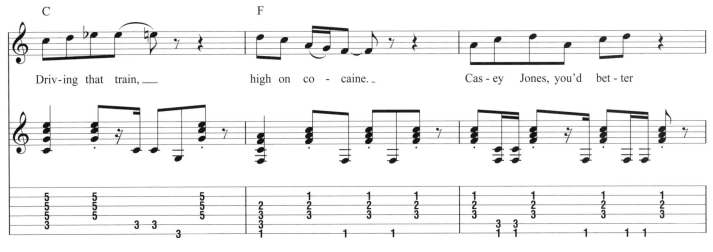

watch your ___ speed. ___ Trou-ble a - head, ___ trou-ble be - hind. ___

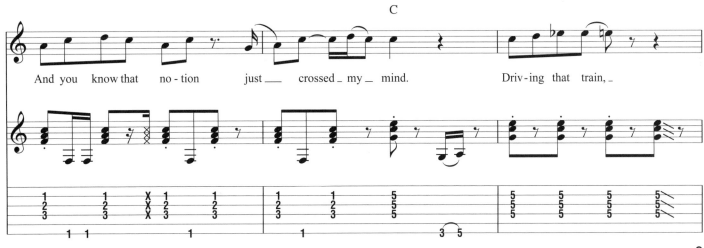

And you know that no - tion just ___ crossed ___ my ___ mind. Driv-ing that train, ___

Sugar Magnolia

Words by Robert Hunter
Music by Bob Weir

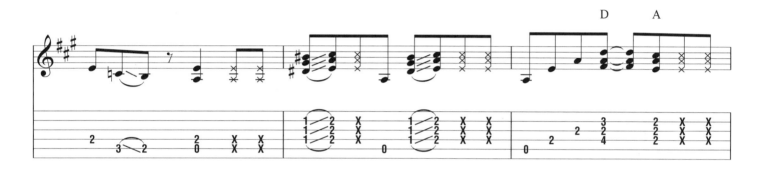

Copyright © 1970 ICE NINE PUBLISHING CO., INC.
Copyright Renewed
All Rights Administered by UNIVERSAL MUSIC CORP.
All Rights Reserved   Used by Permission

don't care. Saw my ba - by down __ by the riv - er, __

knew she had to come up __ soon _ for air. __

Verse

2. Sweet blos - som come on, un - der the wil - low. We can have high _ times if you'll a - bide.

We can dis - cov - er the won - ders of na - ture, __ roll - ing in the rush - es, down __ by the riv - er - side.

Chorus

She's got ev-'ry-thing _ de-light-ful.

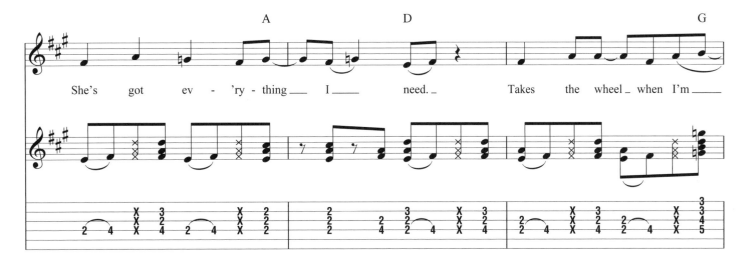

She's got ev-'ry-thing _ I _ need. _ Takes the wheel _ when I'm _____

____ see-ing dou-ble. Pays _ my tick-et when I speed. _____

Pedal Steel Solo

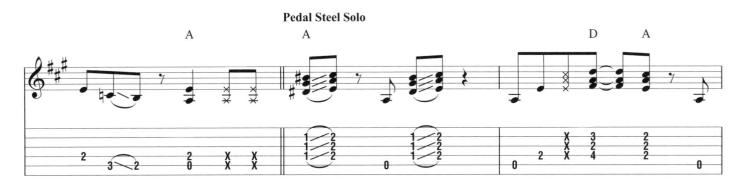

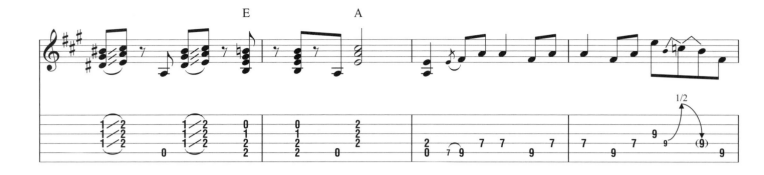

Verse

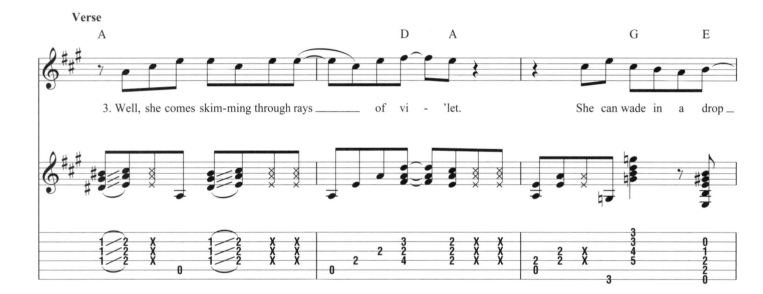

3. Well, she comes skim-ming through rays _____ of vi - 'let. She can wade in a drop _____

_____ of dew. ___ She don't come and I _____ don't _____ fol - low.

Bridge

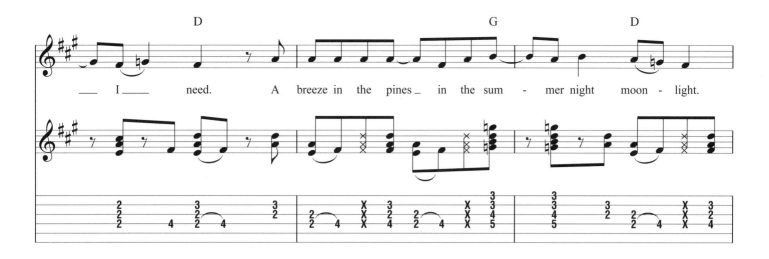

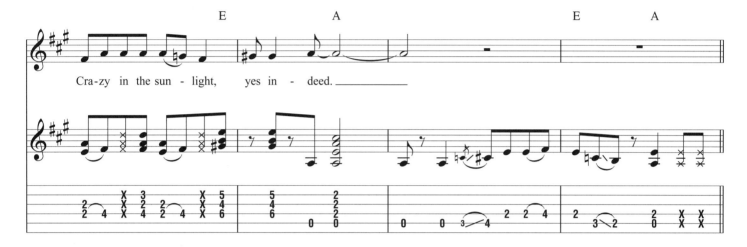

Verse

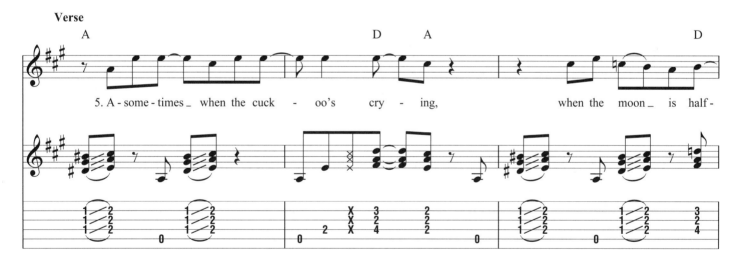

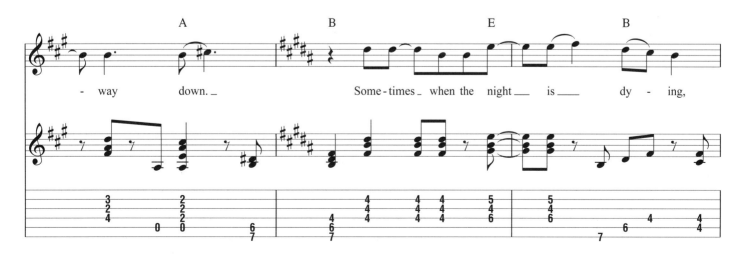

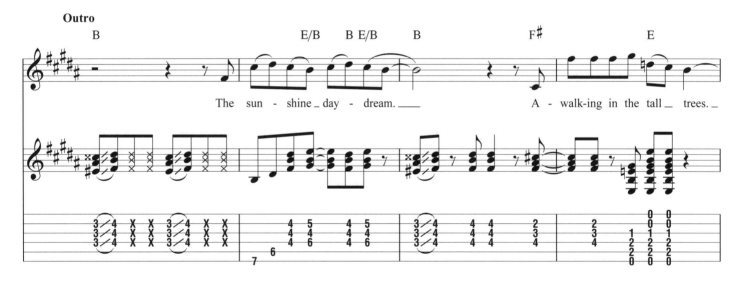

Outro

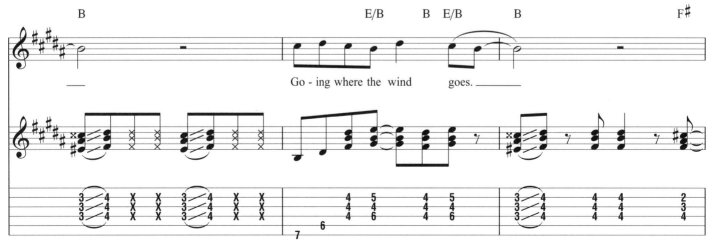

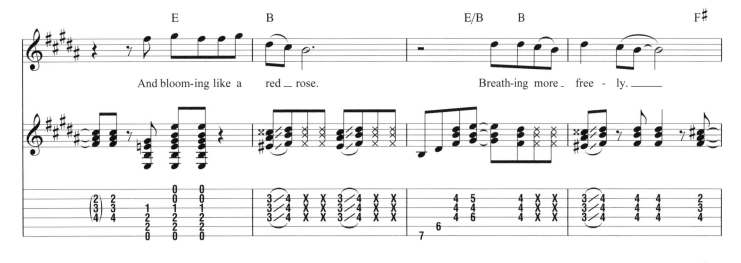

And bloom-ing like a red __ rose. Breath-ing more __ free-ly. ___

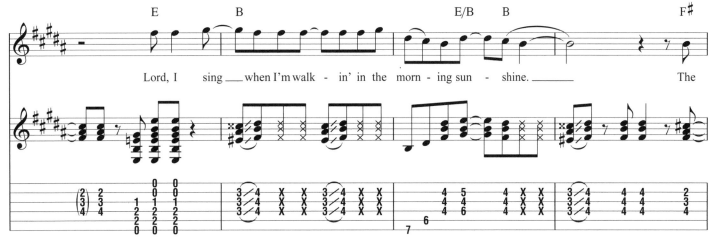

Lord, I sing ___ when I'm walk - in' in the morn - ing sun - shine. _____ The

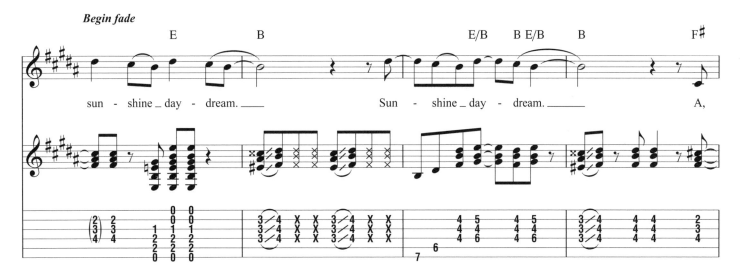

Begin fade

sun - shine __ day - dream. ___ Sun - shine __ day - dream. _____ A,

Fade out

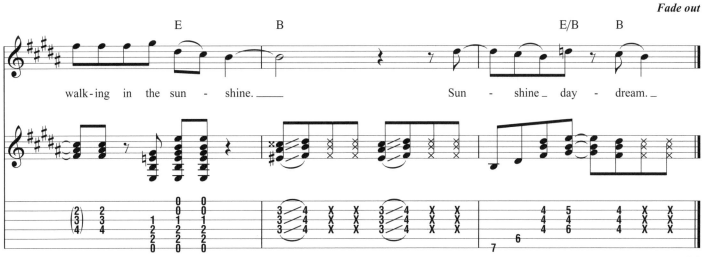

walk-ing in the sun - shine. ___ Sun - shine __ day - dream. __

Easy Wind

Words and Music by Robert Hunter

Copyright © 1970 ICE NINE PUBLISHING CO., INC.
Copyright Renewed
All Rights Administered by UNIVERSAL MUSIC CORP.
All Rights Reserved   Used by Permission

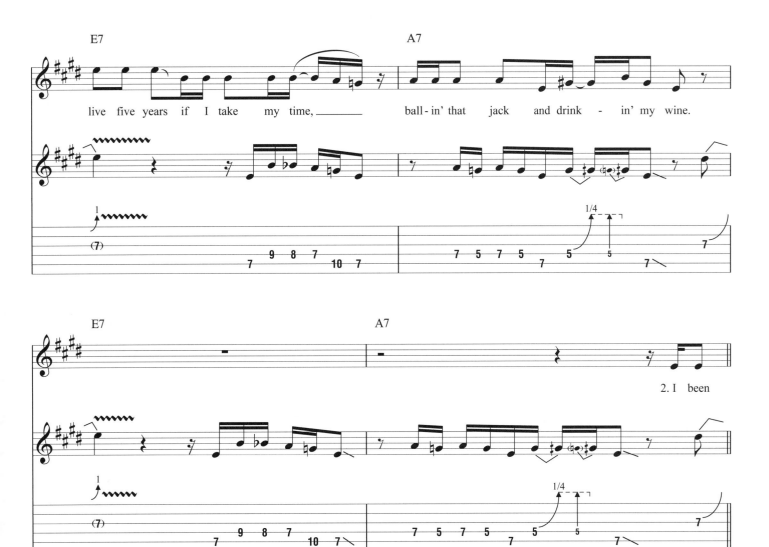

live five years if I take my time, _____ ball-in' that jack and drink - in' my wine.

2. I been

Verse

chip-pin' them rocks from dawn till doom while my rid-er hide my bot-tle in the oth - er room. _____

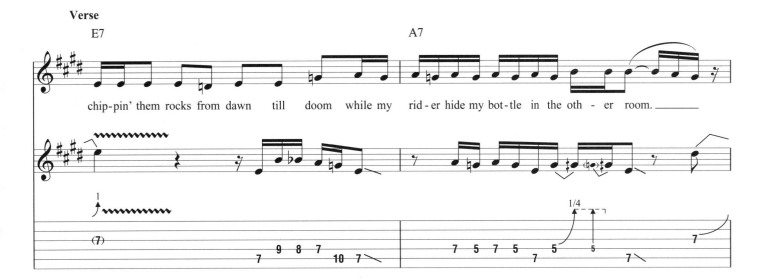

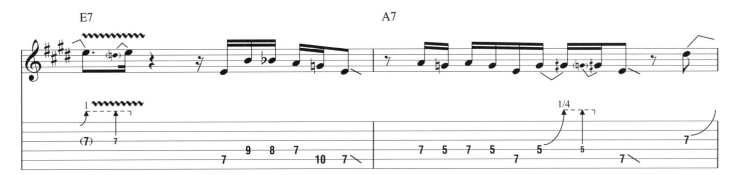

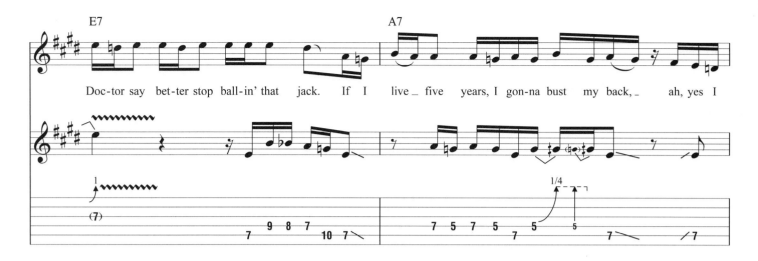

Doc-tor say bet-ter stop ball-in' that jack. If I live _ five years, I gon-na bust my back, _ ah, yes I

Chorus

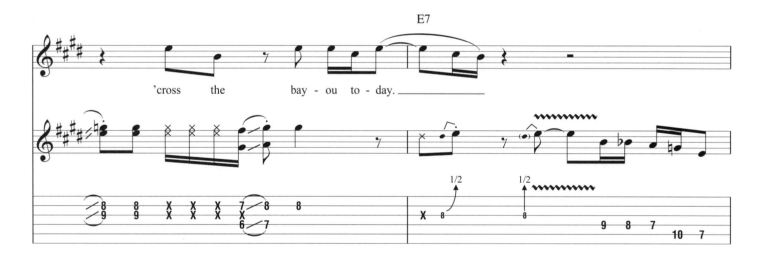

will. _ Eas - y wind _

'cross the bay - ou to - day. _____

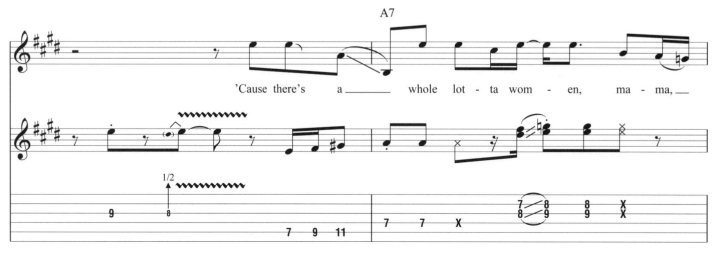

'Cause there's a _____ whole lot - ta wom - en, ma - ma, ___

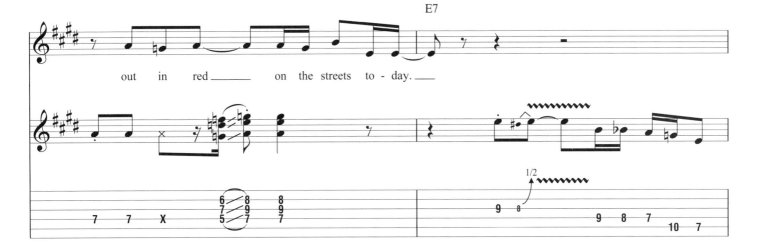

out in red _____ on the streets to - day. _____

And the riv - er keeps a - talk - in', ___ but you

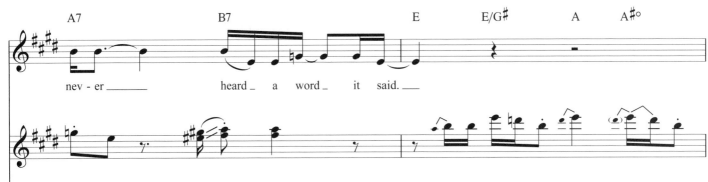

nev - er _____ heard _ a word _ it said. ___

Harmonica Solo

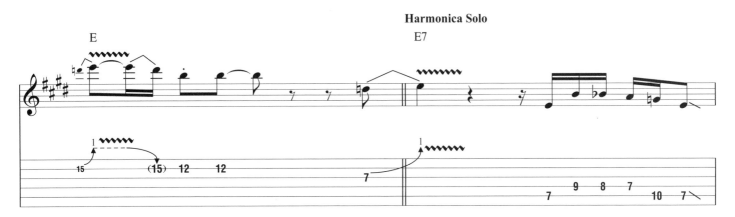

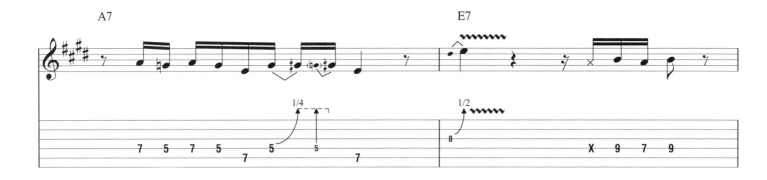

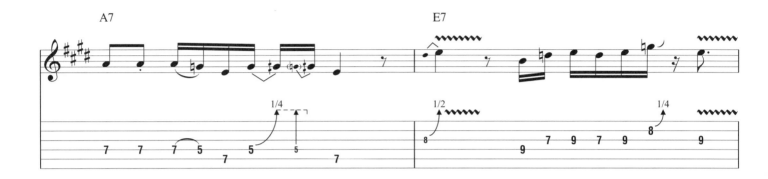

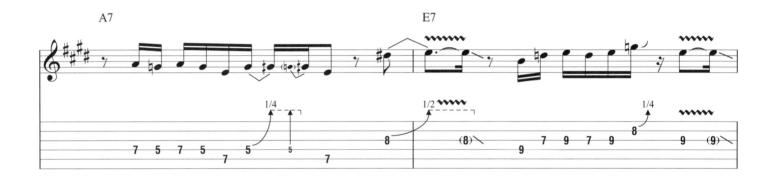

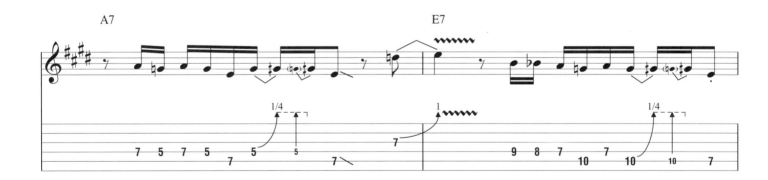

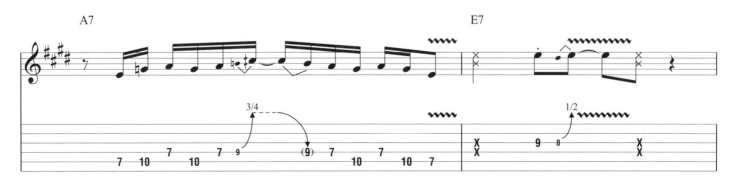

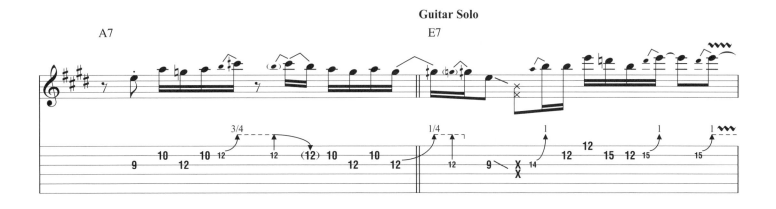

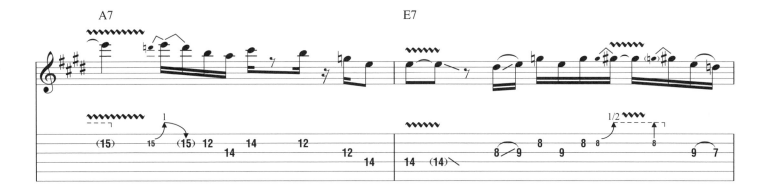

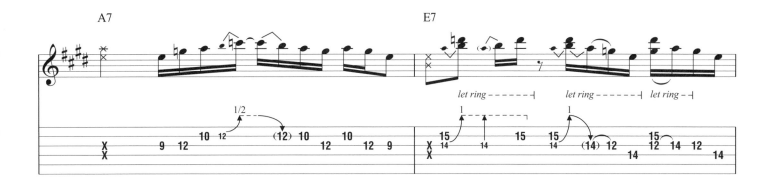

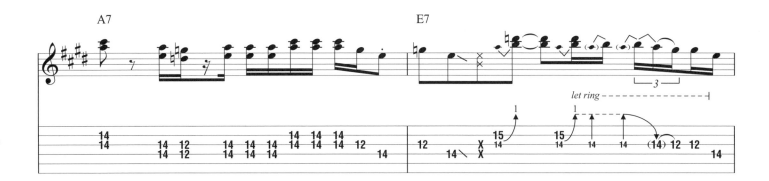

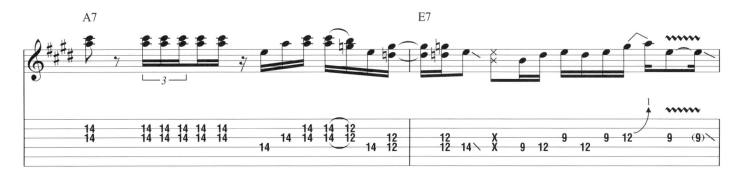

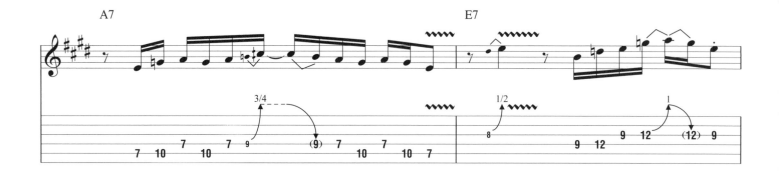

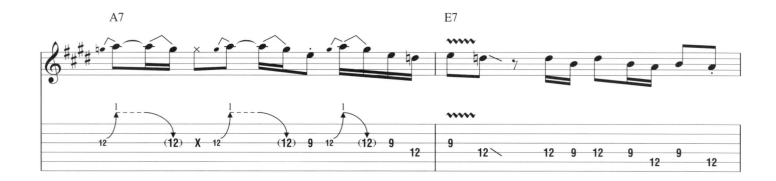

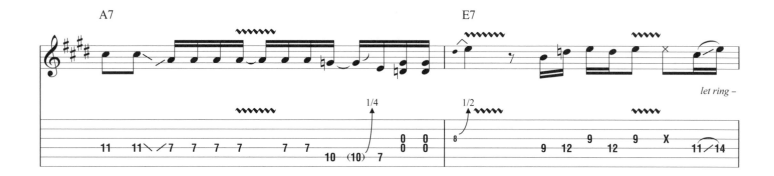

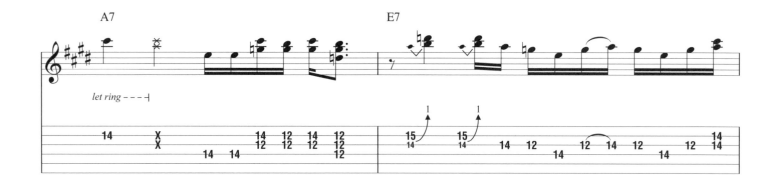

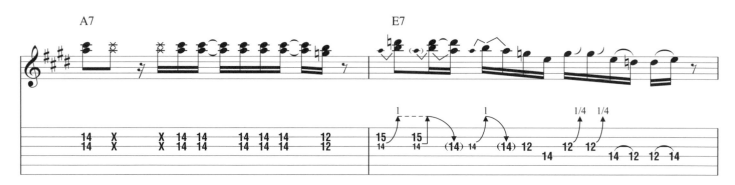

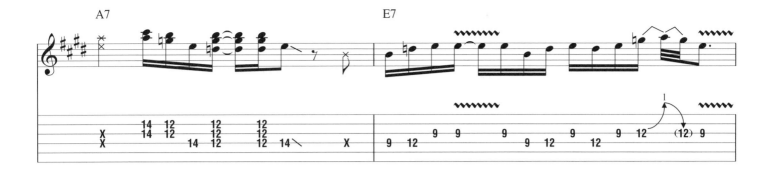

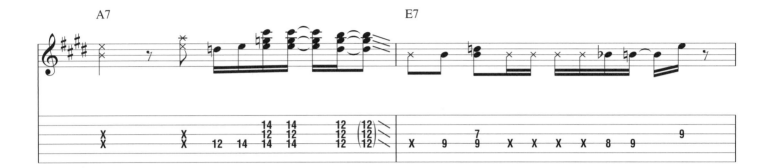

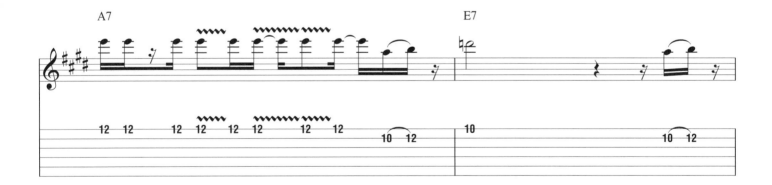

Guitar Solo

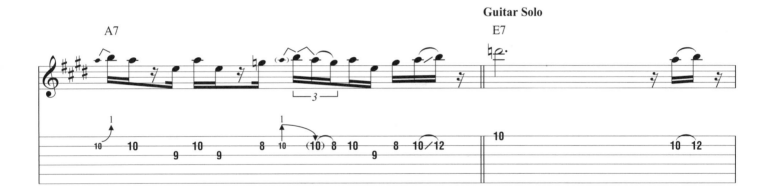

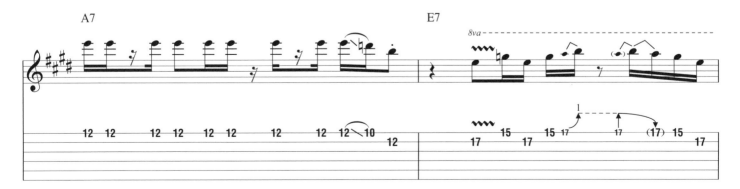

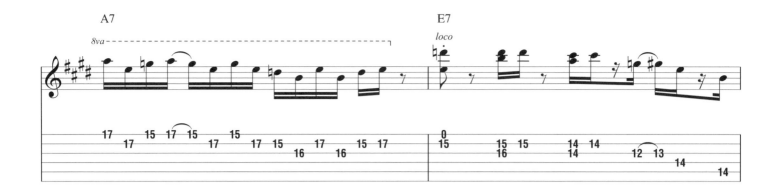

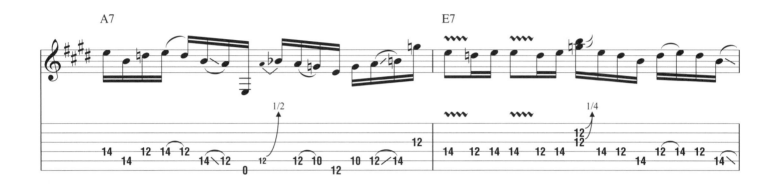

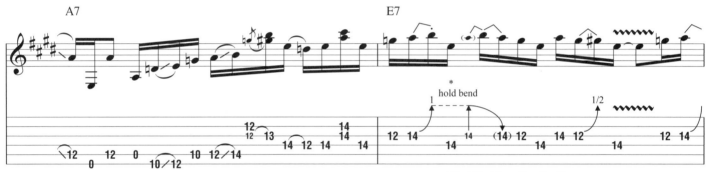

*Fret 4th string w/ bending finger.

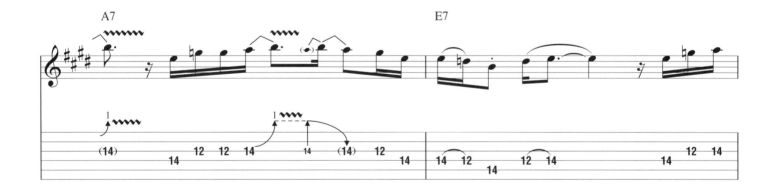

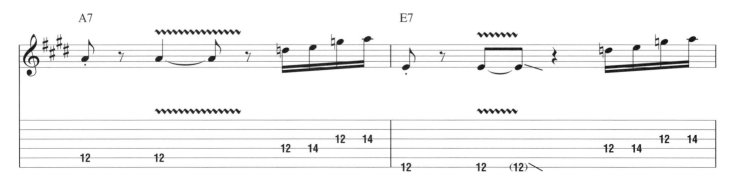

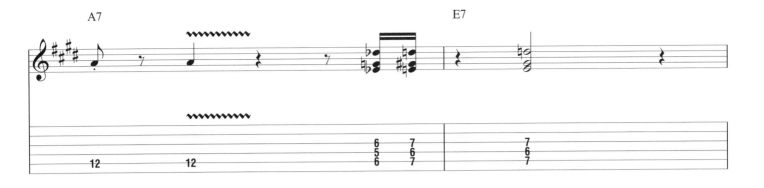

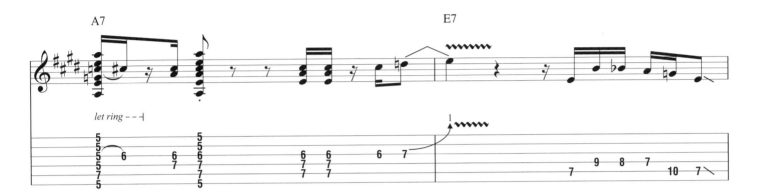

Verse

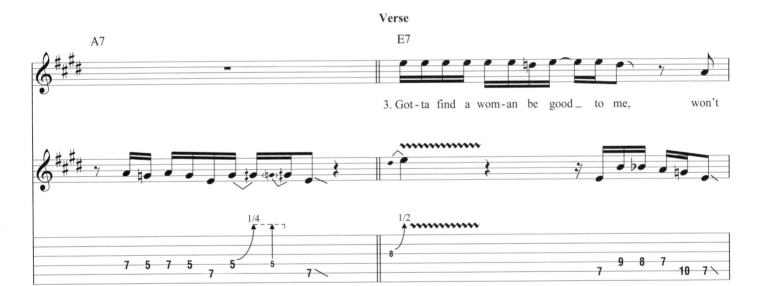

3. Got-ta find a wom-an be good _ to me, won't

hide my li-quor, try to serve me tea. _

'Cause I'm a stone jack ball- er and my heart is true, _____ and I'll

give _ ev-'ry-thing _ that I got to you, _____ yes, I will. _

Outro-Chorus

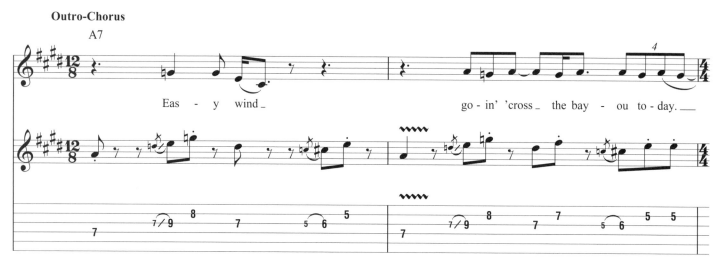

Eas - y wind _ go - in' 'cross _ the bay - ou to - day. __

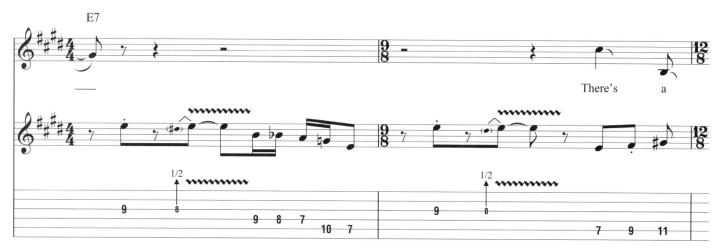

There's a

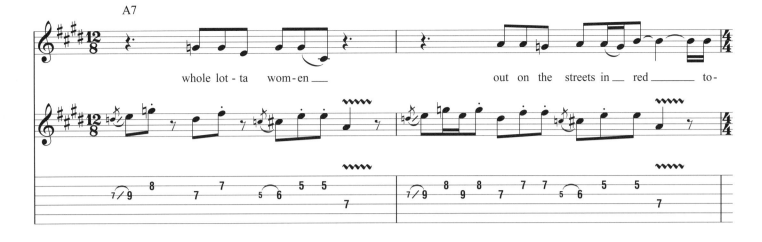

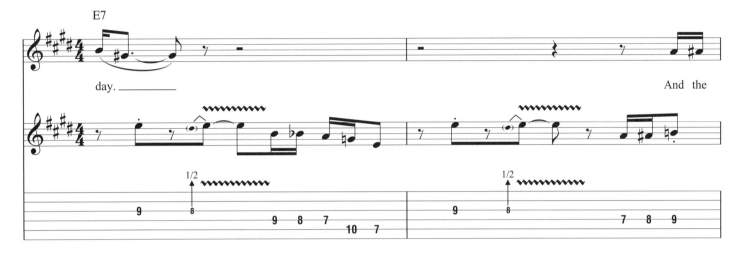

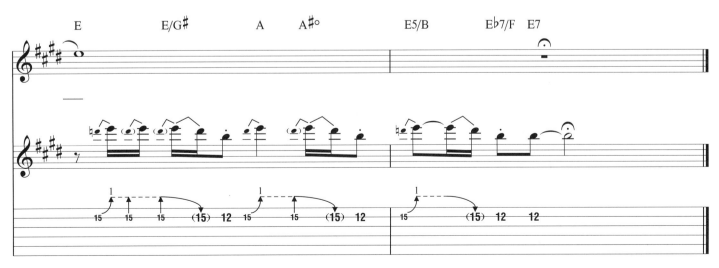

Friend of the Devil

Words by Robert Hunter
Music by Jerry Garcia and John Dawson

Intro
Moderately ♩ = 103

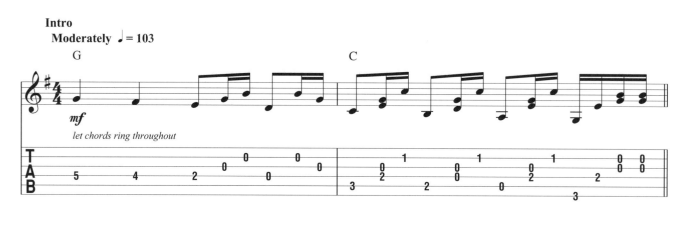

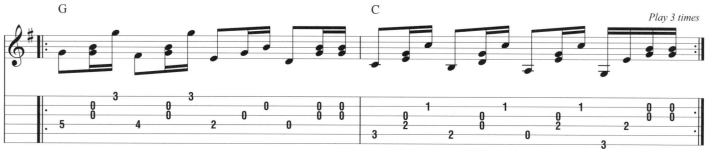

Verse

1. I lit up __ from Re - no, I __ was trailed by twen - ty hounds. __

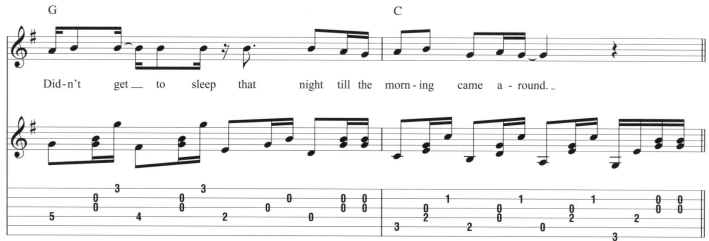

Did-n't get __ to sleep that night till the morn - ing came a - round. __

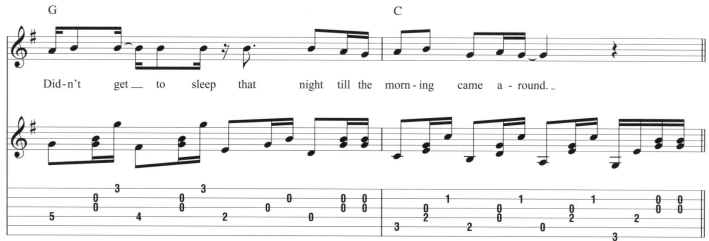

Copyright © 1970 ICE NINE PUBLISHING CO., INC.
Copyright Renewed
All Rights Administered by UNIVERSAL MUSIC CORP.
All Rights Reserved   Used by Permission

Chorus

Set out run-ning but I take my time, ___ a friend of the Dev-il is a ___ friend of mine. ___

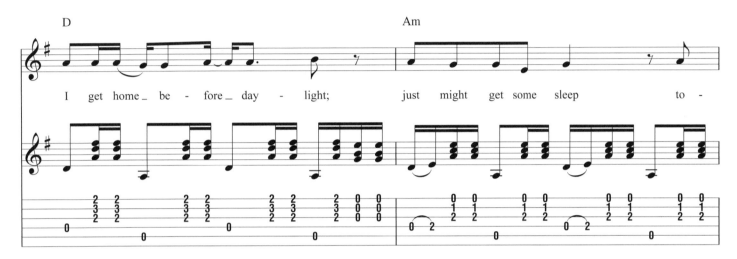

I get home ___ be - fore ___ day - light; just might get some sleep to -

night. _____

Verse

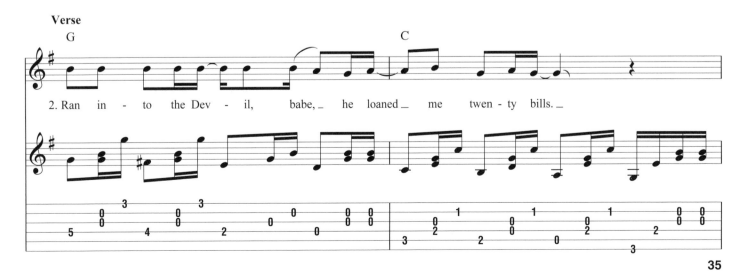

2. Ran in - to the Dev - il, babe, ___ he loaned ___ me twen - ty bills. ___

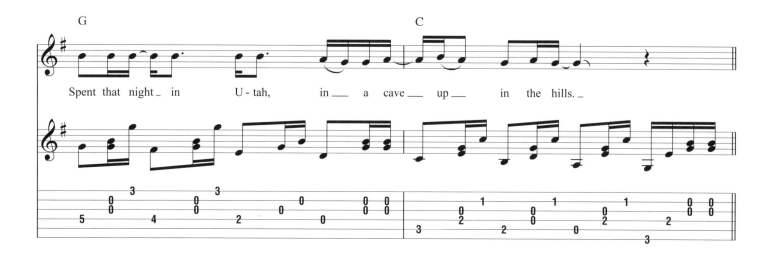

Spent that night _ in U-tah, in _ a cave _ up _ in the hills. _

Chorus

Set out run-ning but I take my time, _ a friend of the Dev-il is a friend of mine. _

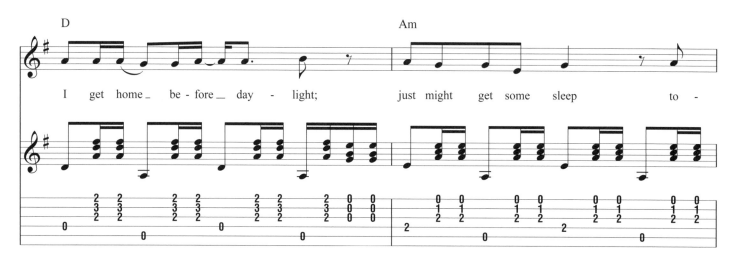

I get home _ be-fore _ day - light; just might get some sleep to -

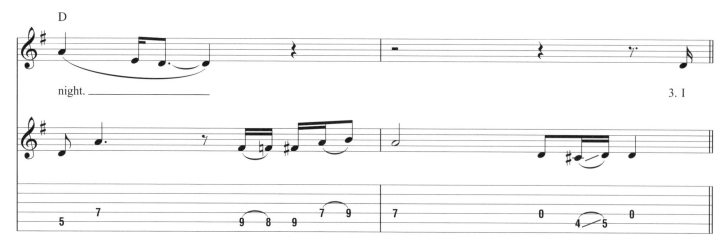

night. _____

3. I

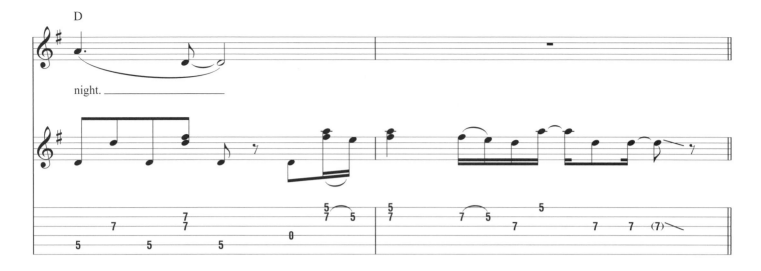

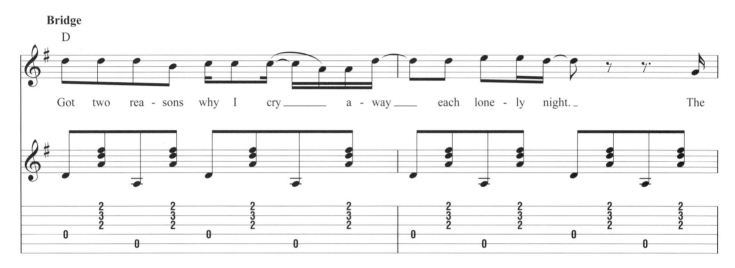

Bridge

Got two rea-sons why I cry ___ a-way ___ each lone-ly night. ___ The

first one's name's sweet Anne Ma-rie ___ and she's ___ my ___ heart's de-light. ___

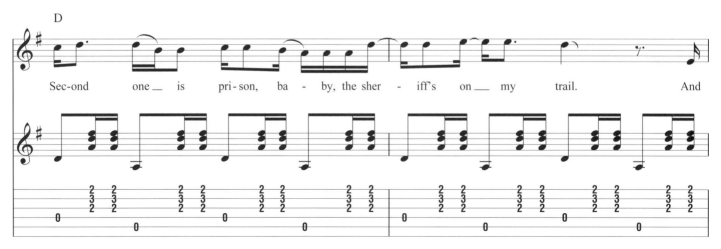

Sec-ond one ___ is pri-son, ba - by, the sher - iff's on ___ my trail. And

if he catch - es up with me ___ I'll spend my life in ___

jail.

Verse

4. Got a wife ___ in Chi - no, babe, ___ and, ah, one in ___ Cher - o - kee. ___

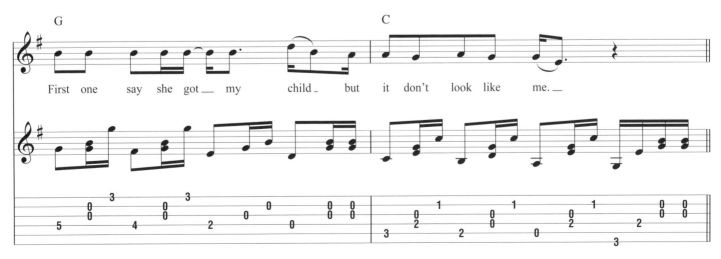

First one say she got ___ my child ___ but it don't look like me. ___

Chorus

Set out run-ning but I take my time,_ a friend of the Dev-il is a friend_ of mine._

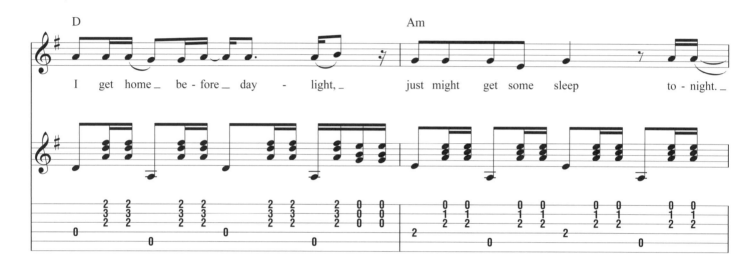

I get home_ be-fore_ day - light,_ just might get some sleep to - night._

Guitar Solo

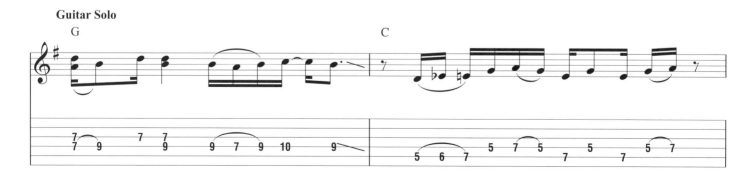

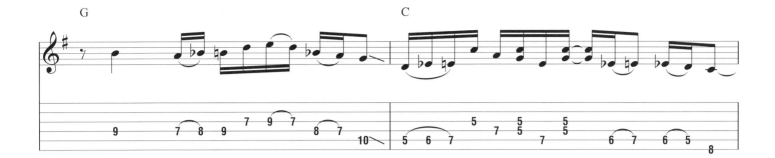

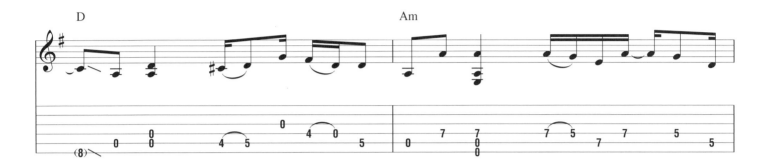

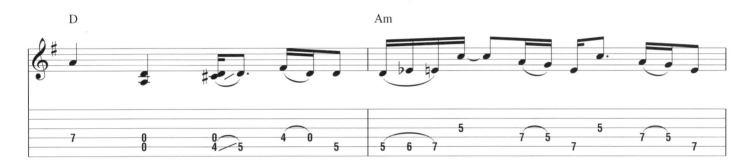

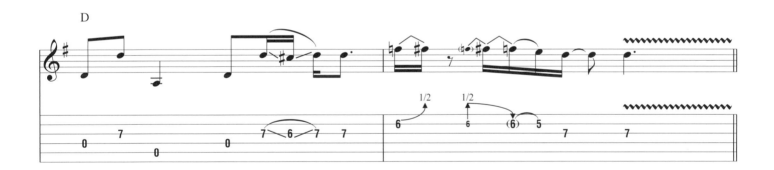

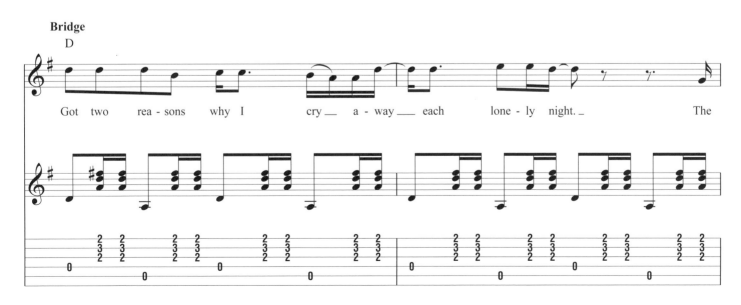

Bridge

Got two rea-sons why I cry __ a-way __ each lone-ly night. __ The

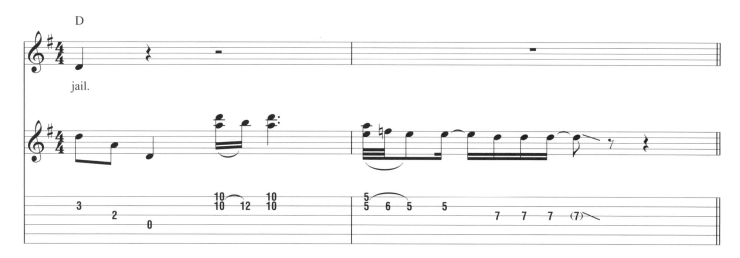

Verse

5. Got a wife _ in Chi - no, babe, _ and, ah, one in Cher - o - kee. _

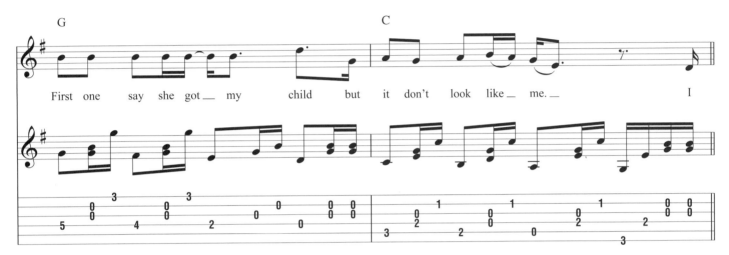

First one say she got _ my child but it don't look like _ me. _ I

Chorus

set out run-nin' but I take my time, a friend of the Dev-il is a friend _ of mine. _

I get home _ be-fore _ day - light, just might get some sleep to - night. _____

Ripple

Words by Robert Hunter
Music by Jerry Garcia

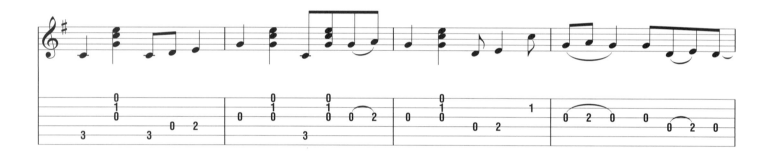

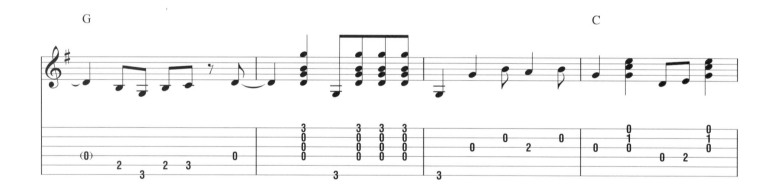

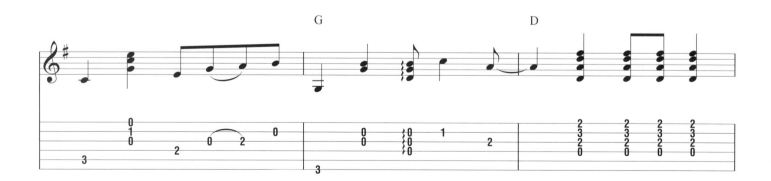

Copyright © 1971 ICE NINE PUBLISHING CO., INC.
Copyright Renewed
All Rights Administered by UNIVERSAL MUSIC CORP.
All Rights Reserved   Used by Permission

Verse

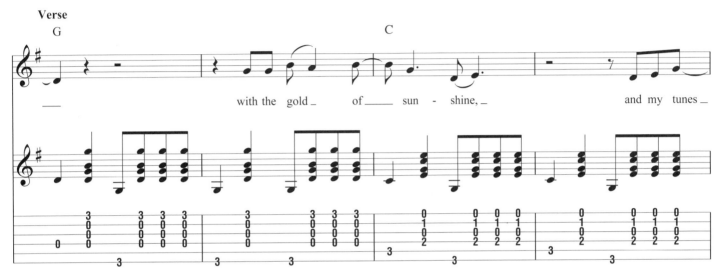

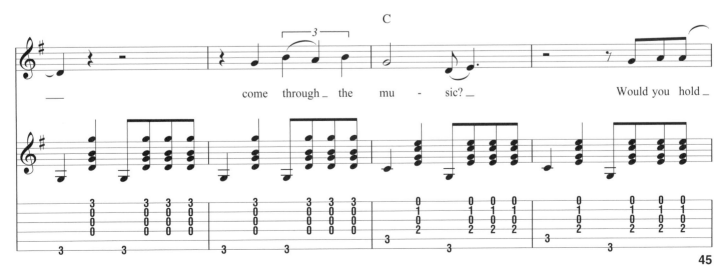

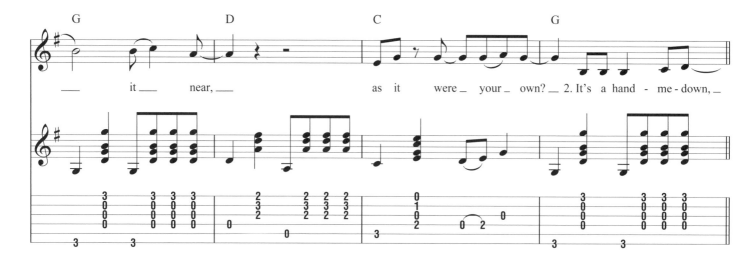

Verse

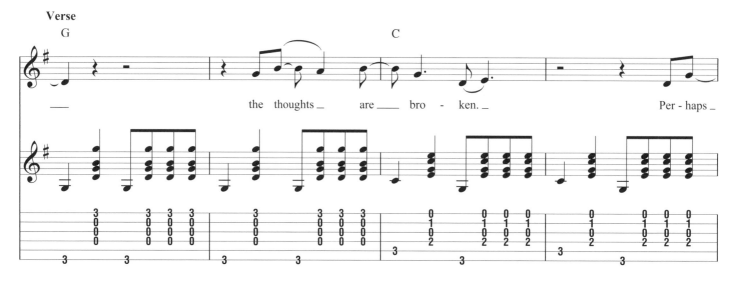

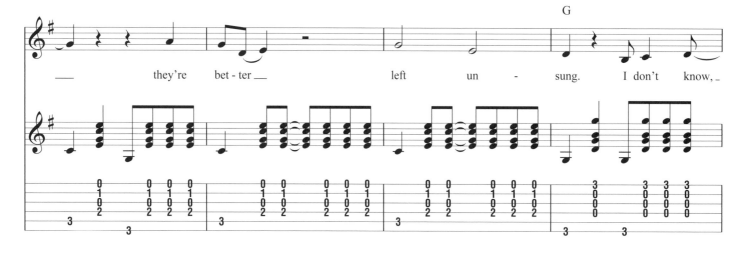

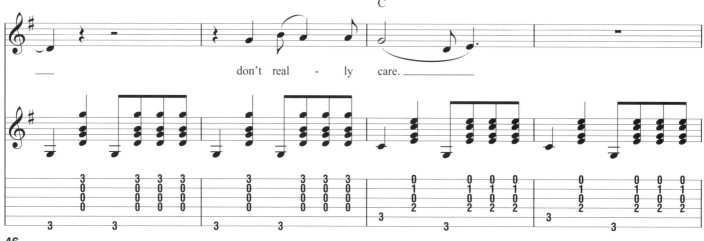

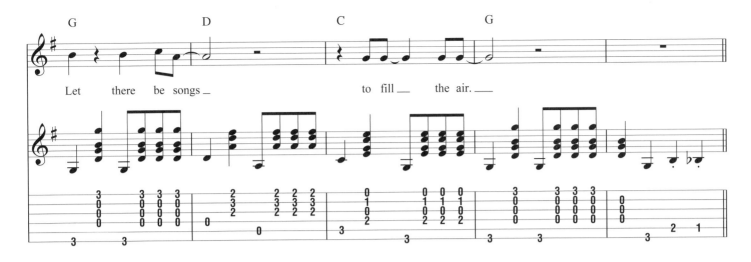

Chorus

Verse

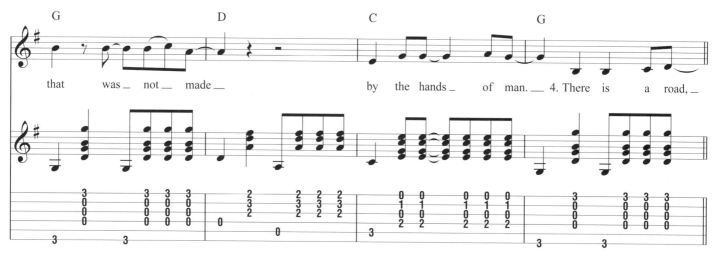

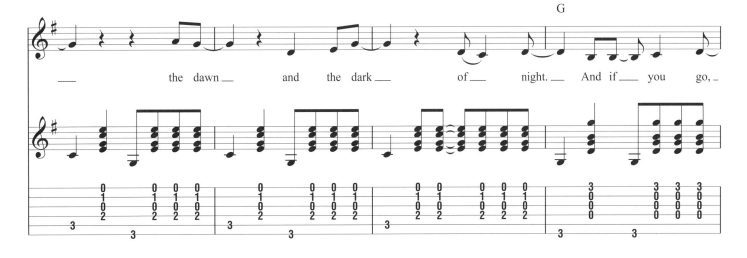

the dawn ___ and the dark ___ of ___ night. ___ And if ___ you go, ___

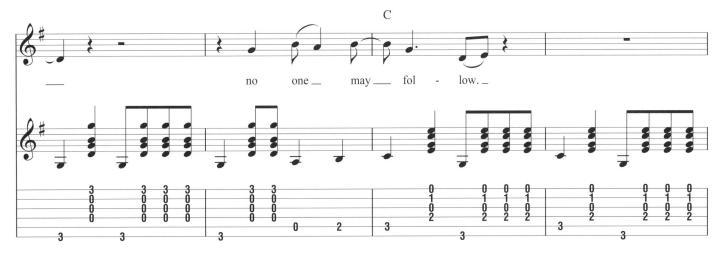

no one ___ may ___ fol - low. ___

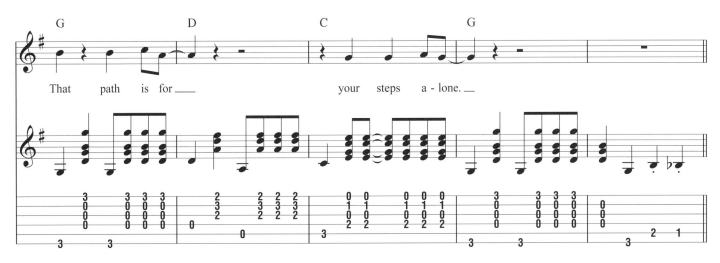

That path is for ___ your steps a - lone. ___

Chorus

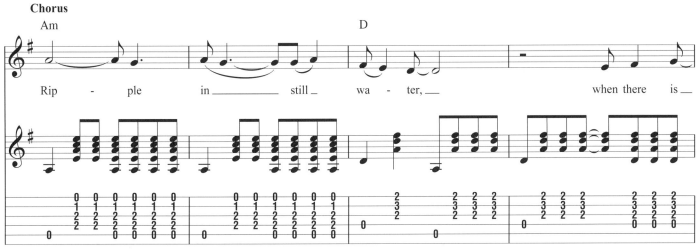

Rip - ple in ___ still ___ wa - ter, ___ when there is ___

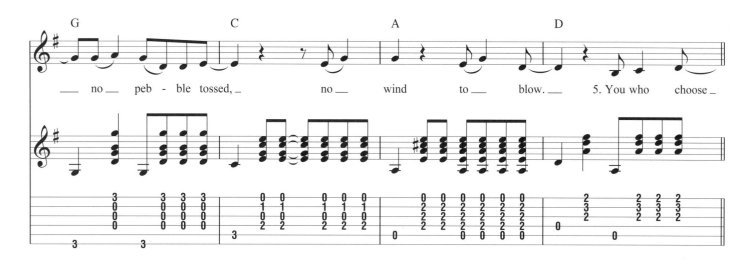

Verse

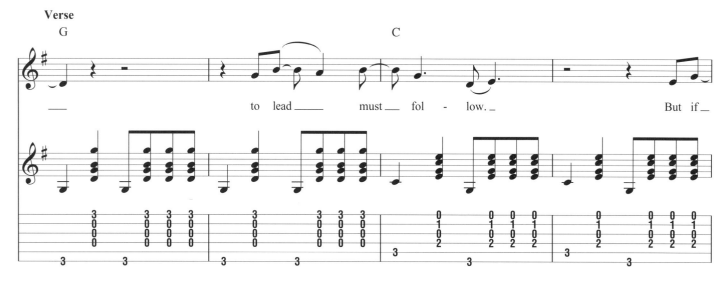

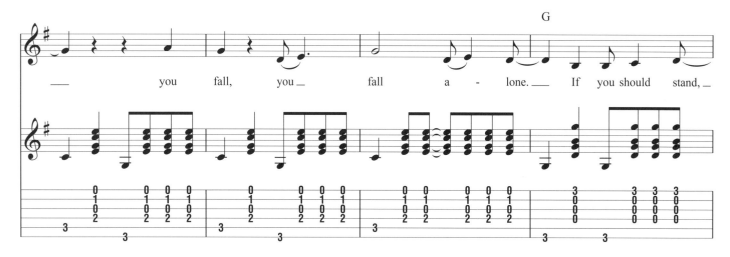

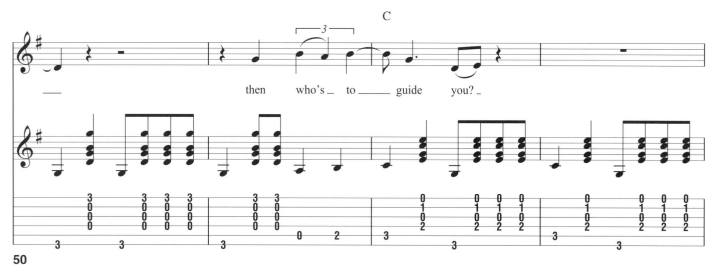

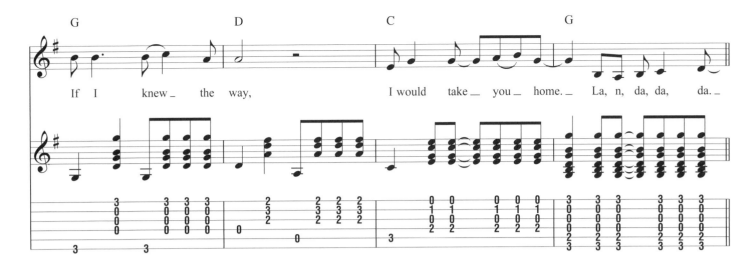

Outro

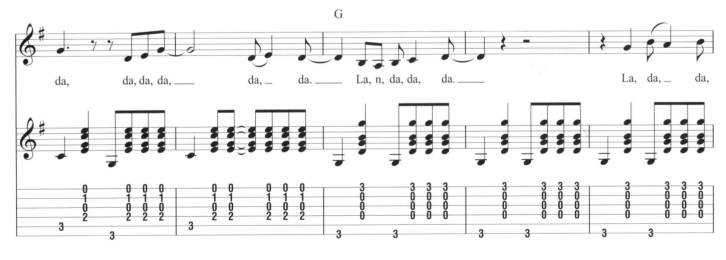

Truckin'

Words by Robert Hunter
Music by Jerry Garcia, Phil Lesh and Bob Weir

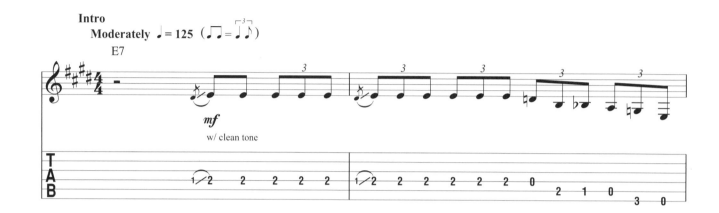

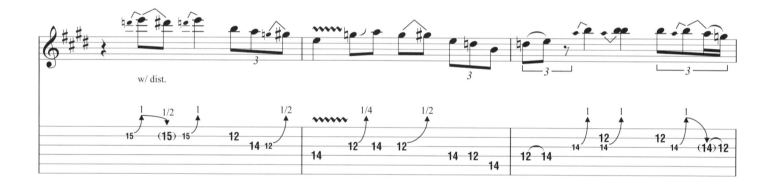

Copyright © 1971 ICE NINE PUBLISHING CO., INC.
Copyright Renewed
All Rights Administered by UNIVERSAL MUSIC CORP.
All Rights Reserved   Used by Permission

truck-in',   like the doo-dah ___ man. ___   To - geth - er,   more or

let chords ring throughout

less in ___ line. ___   Just keep truck-in' on. _____

P.M.   P.M.   P.M.

Verse

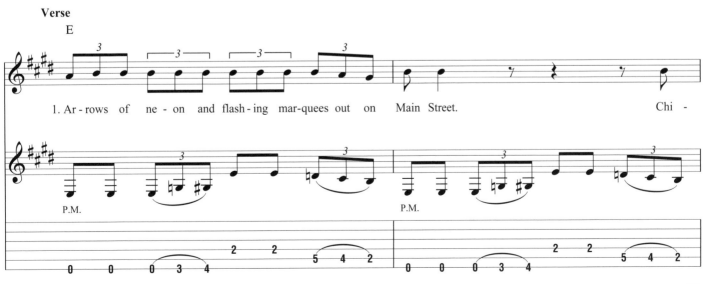

1. Ar - rows of ne - on and flash - ing mar-quees out on Main Street.   Chi -

P.M.   P.M.

ca - go, New York, De - troit and it's all on the same street. ___ Your

typ - i - cal cit - y in - volved in a typ - i - cal day dream,

hang it up and see what to - mor - row brings. ___

Chorus

Dal - las got a soft ma - chine. ___ Hous - ton, too close to

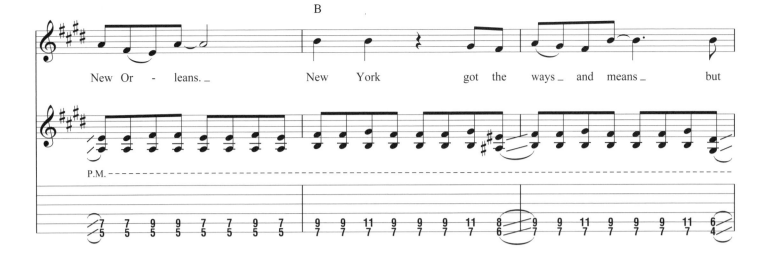

New Or - leans. _ New York got the ways _ and means _ but

just won't let _ you be. _____

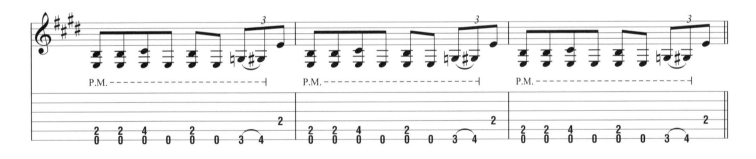

Verse

2. Most of the cats that you meet on the street speak of true love,

most of the time they're sit - ting and cry - ing at home.

One of these days, they know they got - ta get go - ing

out of that door and down to the street all a - lone.____

Chorus

E   A

Truck - in', like the doo - dah____ man____ once told me you got to

play your __ hand. __   Some - times   the cards ain't worth a dime _____

if you don't lay __ 'em __ down. _____

w/ dist.

dist. off

Some - times   the light's   all   shin - ing   on   me.

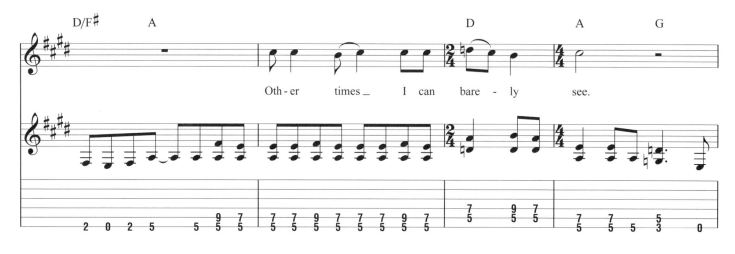

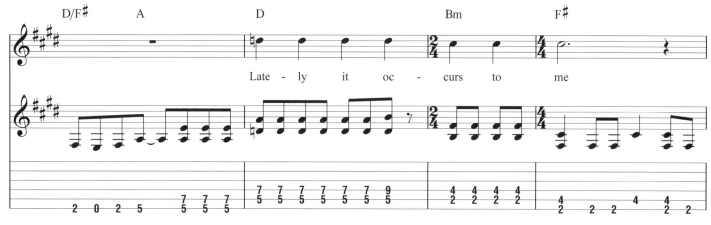

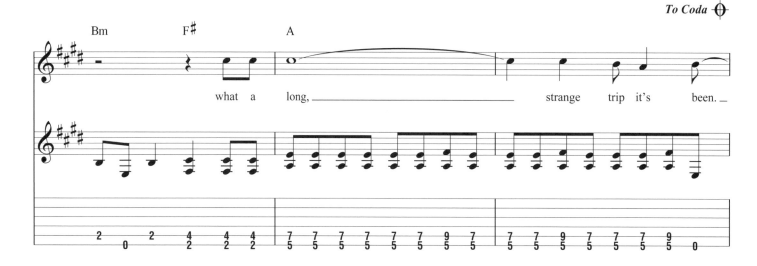

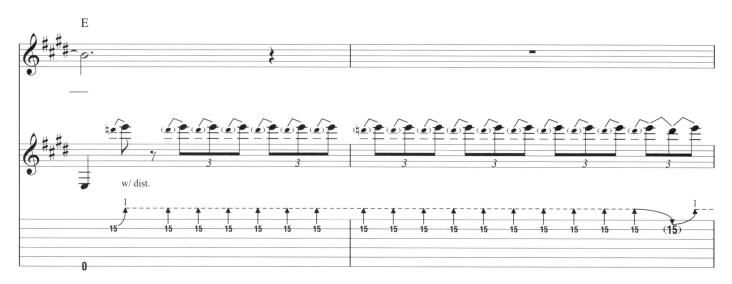

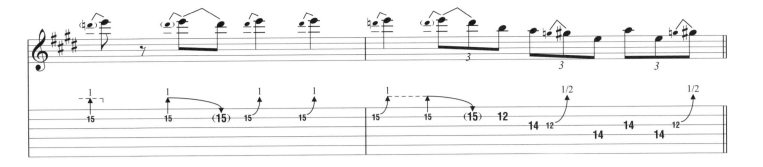

Verse

E

3. What in the world ev - er be - came _ of Sweet Jane? _ She lost her spark-le, you know she is - n't the

same. Liv-ing on reds, vit - a - min C _ and co - caine, _

all a friend can say is ain't it a shame. _

Chorus

Truck-in' off to Buf-fa-lo, ___ been think-in' you got to

mel-low ___ slow. _ Takes time to pick a place _ to go, and

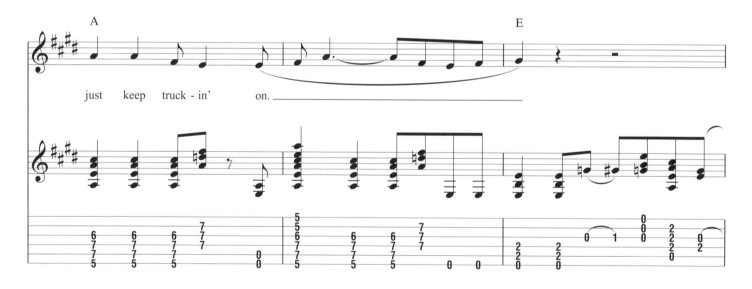

just keep truck-in' on. _____

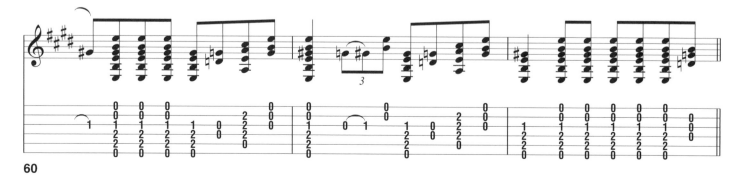

Verse

4. Sit - ting and star - ing out of the ho - tel win - dow, ___

got a tip they're gon - na kick the door in ___ a - gain. I'd

like to get some sleep be - fore ___ I trav - el, ___ but if

you've got a war - rant, I guess you're gon - na come in. ___

Bust - ed   down on Bour-bon __ Street, __   set up   like a

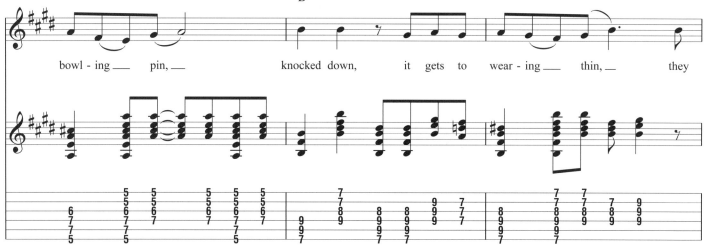

bowl - ing __ pin, __   knocked down,   it gets to   wear-ing __ thin, __   they

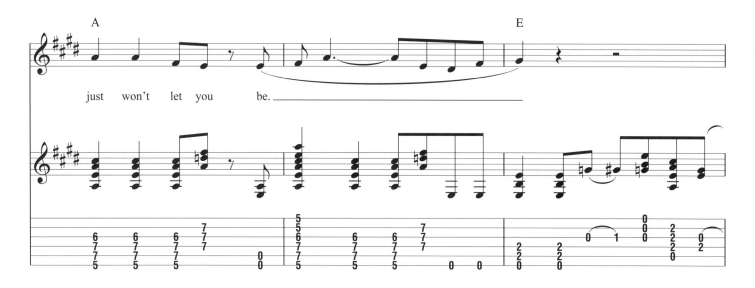

just won't let you   be. _____

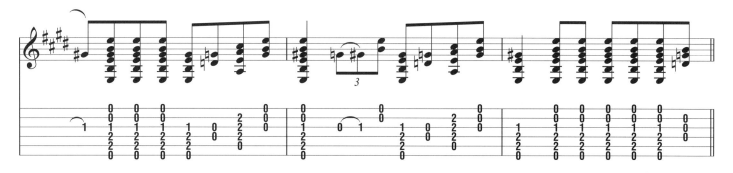

Verse

5. You're sick of hang-ing a-round and you'd like to trav-el, get

tired of trav-el-ing, you want to set-tle down. __ I

guess they can't re-voke __ your soul for try'n'. Get

out of the door, light out and look all a-round. __

D.S. al Coda

⊕ Coda

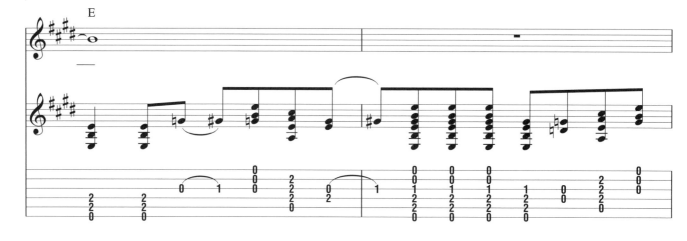

Chorus

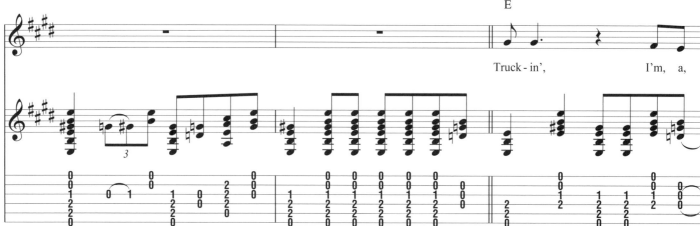

Truck - in', I'm, a,

go - ing _____ home. _____ Woah, woah, ba - by, back where

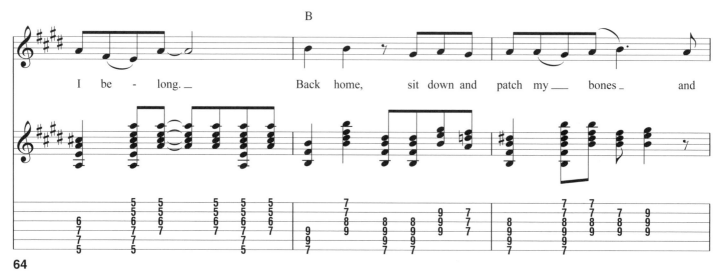

I be - long. _____ Back home, sit down and patch my _____ bones _____ and

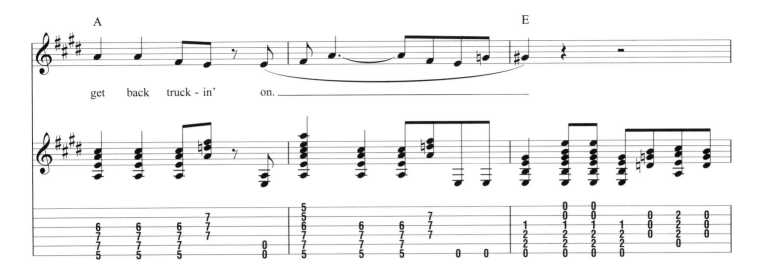

get   back   truck - in'   on. _____

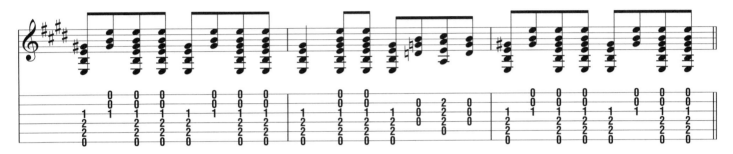

Outro

w/ dist.

Begin fade

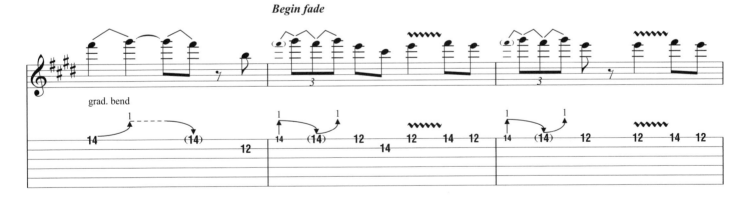

grad. bend

Fade out

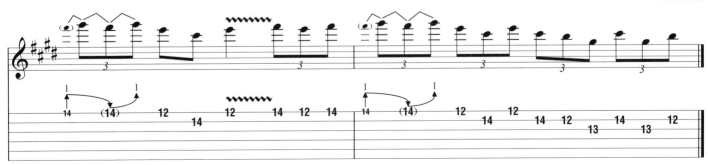

Uncle John's Band

Words by Robert Hunter
Music by Jerry Garcia

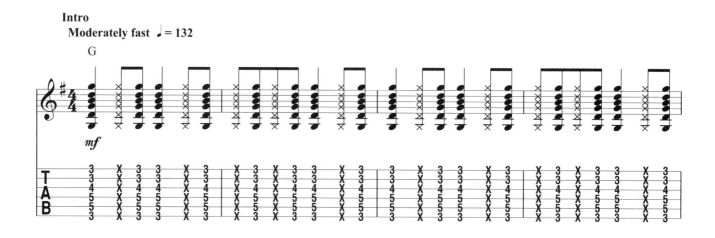

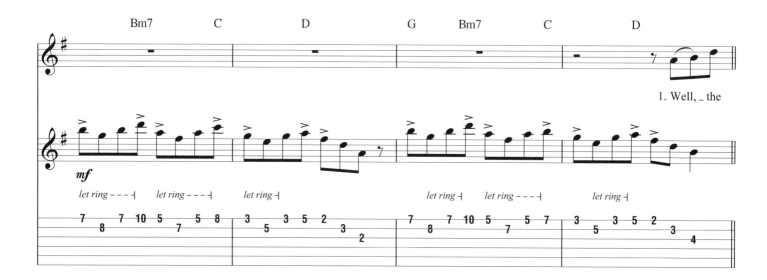

1. Well, _ the

first days _ are _ the hard-est days. _ Don't you wor-ry an-y-more,   'cause _

2. *See additional lyrics*

Copyright © 1970 ICE NINE PUBLISHING CO., INC.
Copyright Renewed
All Rights Administered by UNIVERSAL MUSIC CORP.
All Rights Reserved   Used by Permission

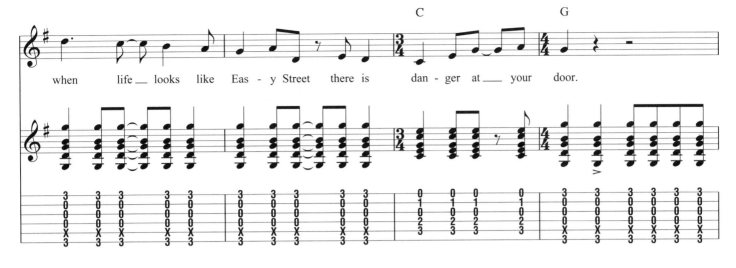

when life __ looks like Eas - y Street there is dan-ger at __ your door.

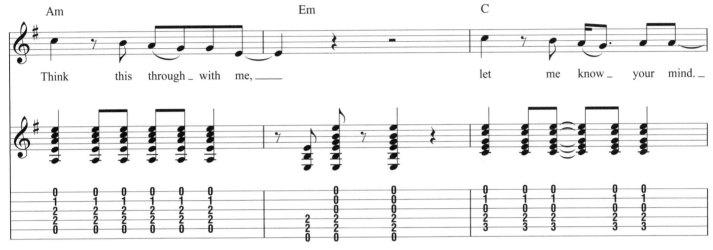

Think this through __ with me, _____ let me know_ your mind. __

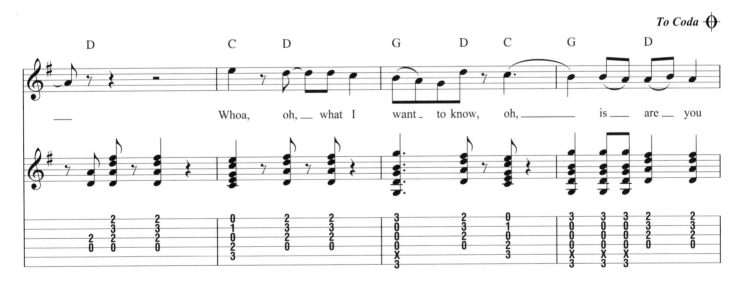

To Coda ⊕

Whoa, oh, __ what I want __ to know, oh, _____ is __ are __ you

D.S. al Coda

kind?   2. It's __ a

Coda

with me?

Chorus

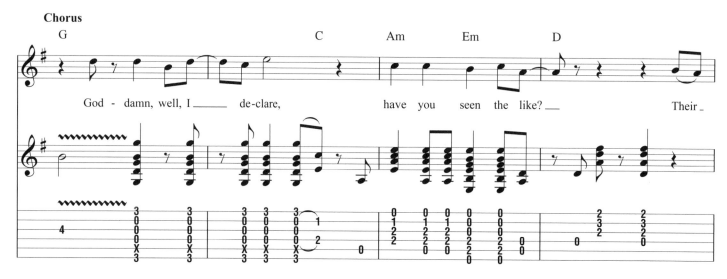

God - damn, well, I _____ de-clare,   have you   seen   the   like? ___   Their _

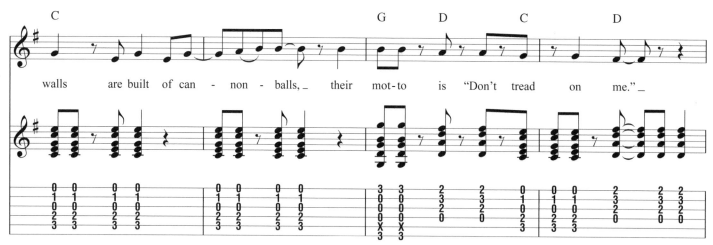

walls   are built of can - non - balls, _   their   mot-to   is   "Don't   tread   on   me." _

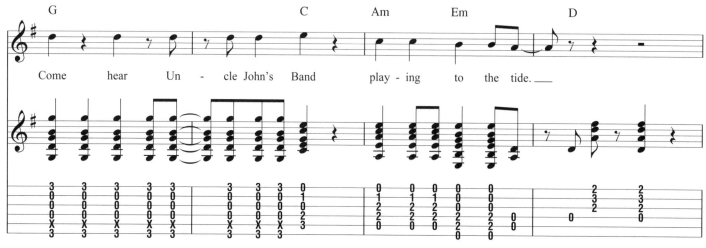

Come   hear   Un - cle John's   Band   play - ing   to   the   tide. ___

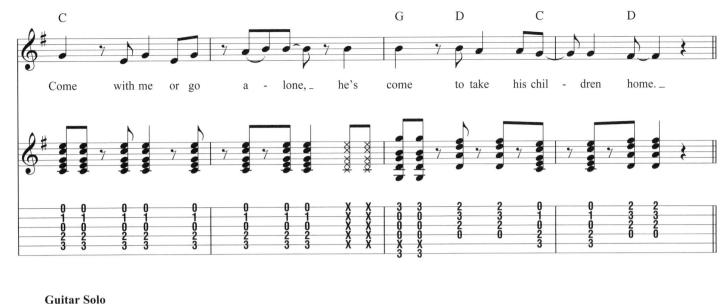

Come with me or go a - lone,__ he's come to take his chil - dren home.__

Guitar Solo

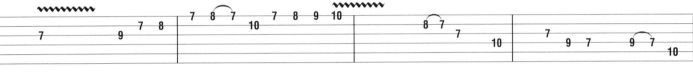

3. It's __

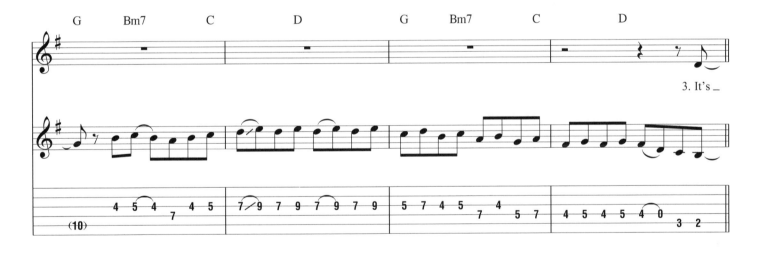

Verse

__ the same sto - ry the crow told me;__ it's the on - ly one __ he knows.

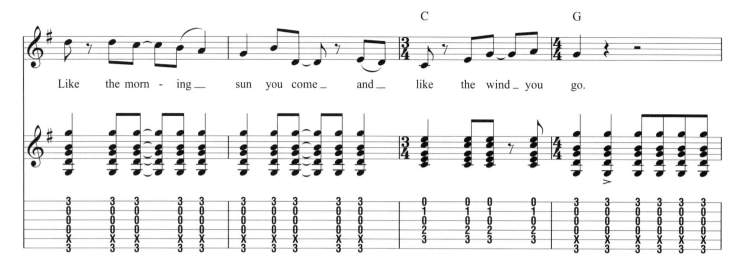

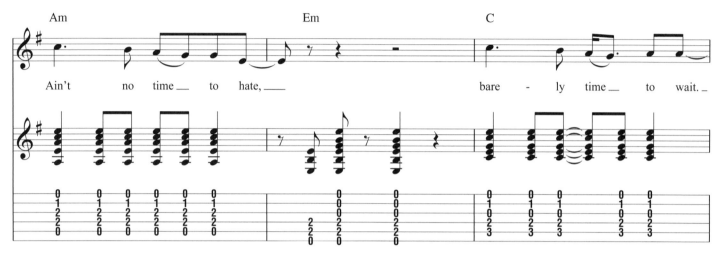

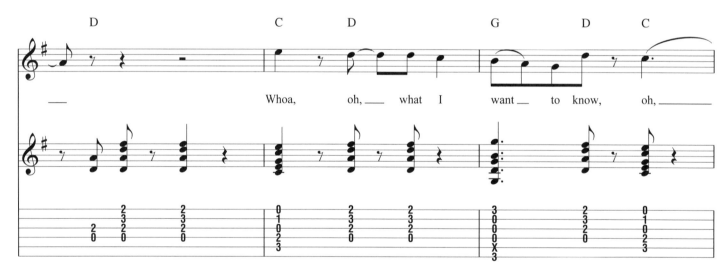

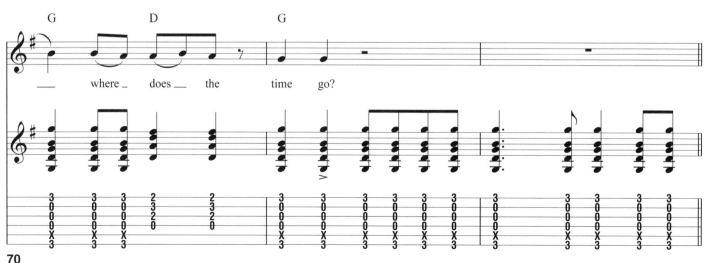

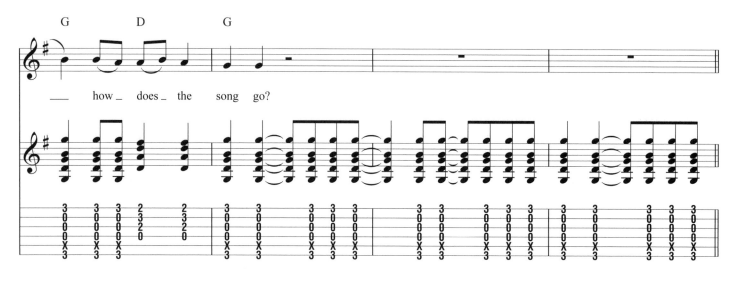

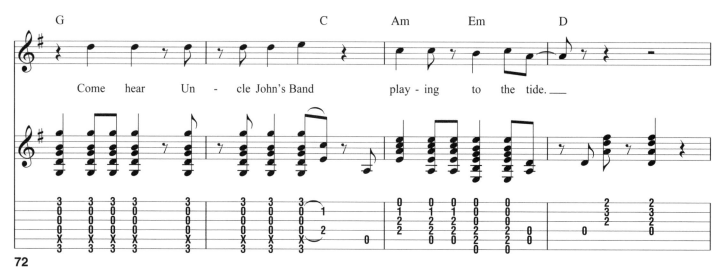

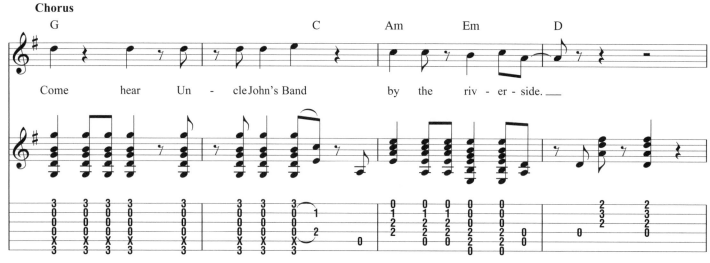

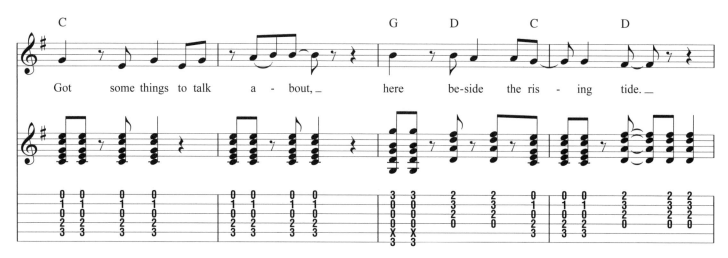

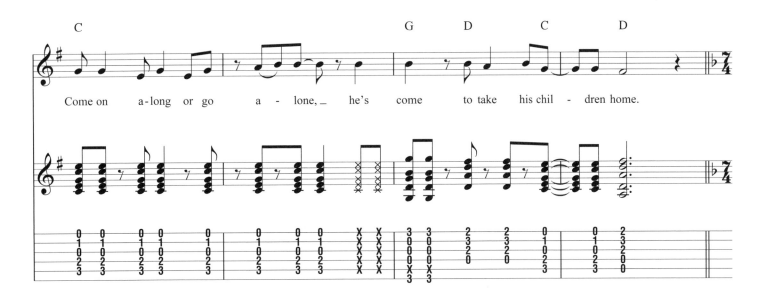

Come on a-long or go a - lone, he's come to take his chil - dren home.

Interlude

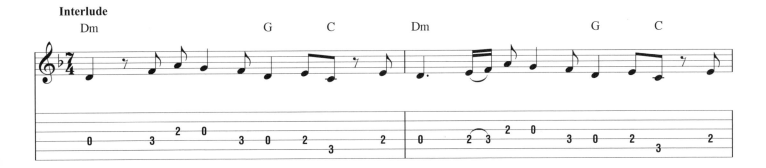

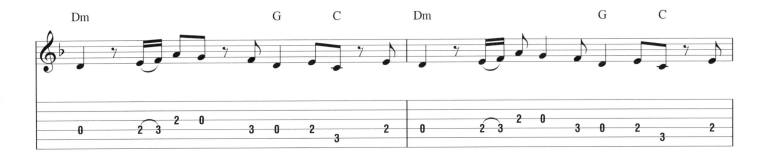

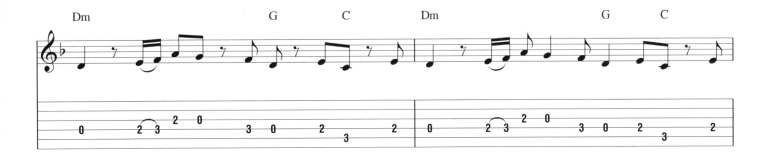

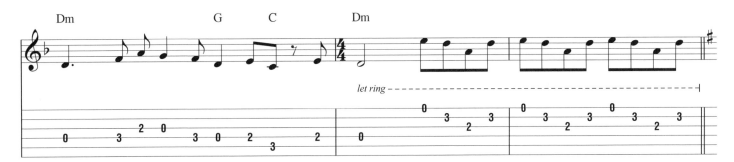

Outro

Da, da, da, da, da, da.
(Oo, _____ da.
Da, da, da, da, da,
Da, da, da, da, da,

da.
da, da, da.
Da, da, da, da, da, da.
Da, da, da, da, da, hey.)

Additional Lyrics

2. It's a buck dancer's choice my friends; better take my advice.
   You know all the rules by now and the fire from the ice.
   Will you come with me? Won't you come with me?
   Whoa, oh, what I want to know, will you come with me.

Touch of Grey

Words by Robert Hunter
Music by Jerry Garcia

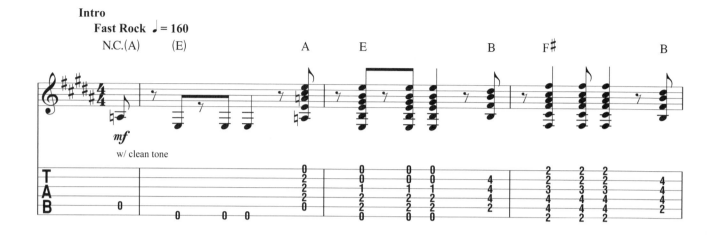

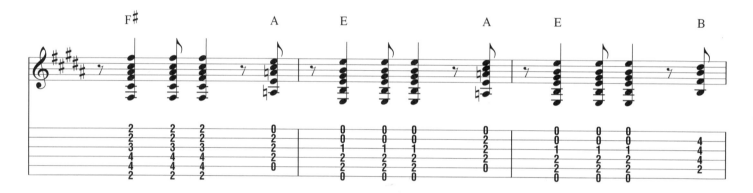

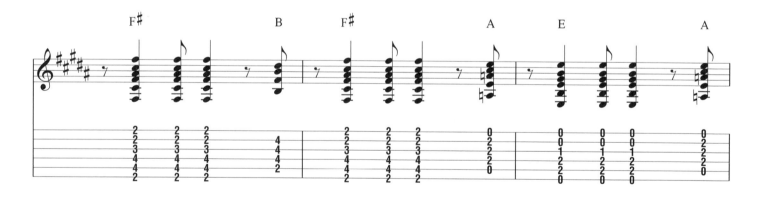

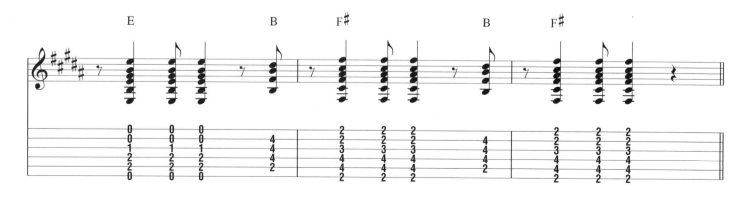

Copyright © 1987 ICE NINE PUBLISHING CO., INC.
All Rights Administered by UNIVERSAL MUSIC CORP.
All Rights Reserved   Used by Permission

Verse

1. It must be get - ting ear - ly, __ clocks are run - ning late,

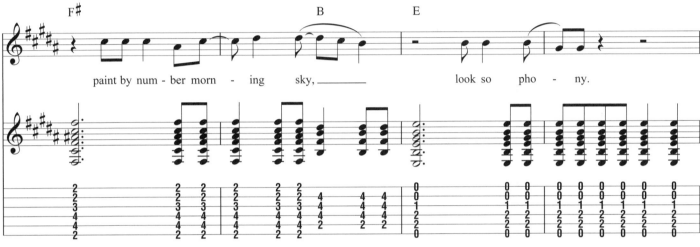

paint by num - ber morn - ing sky, _____ look so pho - ny.

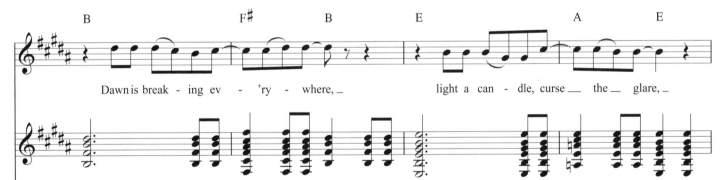

Dawn is break - ing ev - 'ry - where, _ light a can - dle, curse __ the __ glare, _

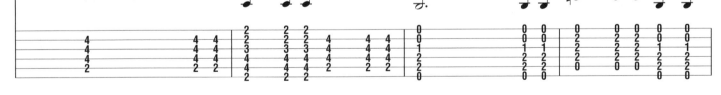

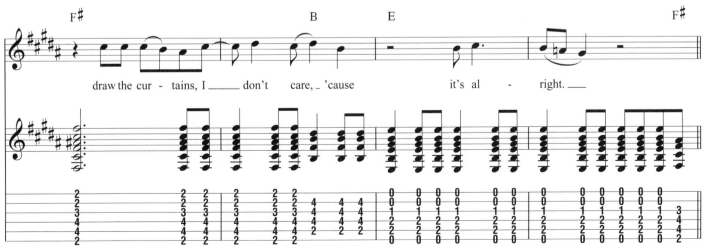

draw the cur - tains, I ____ don't care, _ 'cause it's al - right. ___

Chorus

I will _____ get by, _____

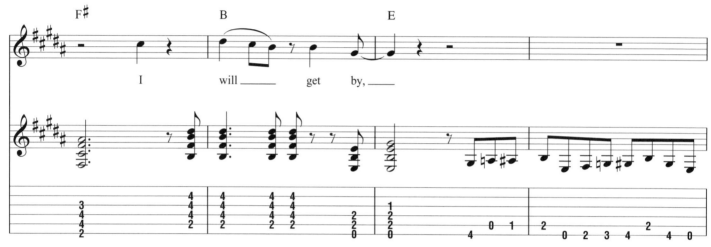

I will _____ get by, _____

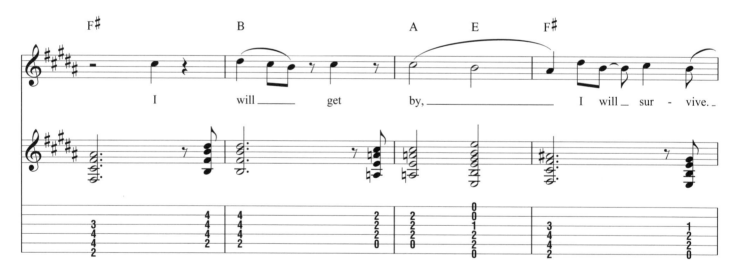

I will _____ get by, _____ I will __ sur - vive. __

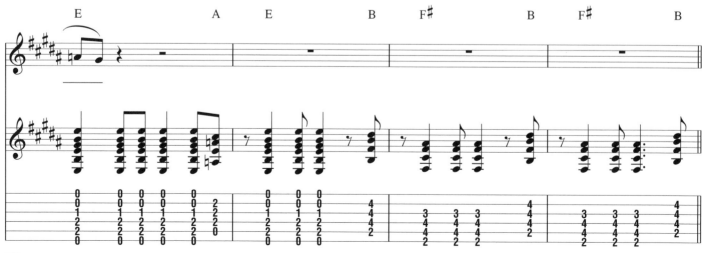

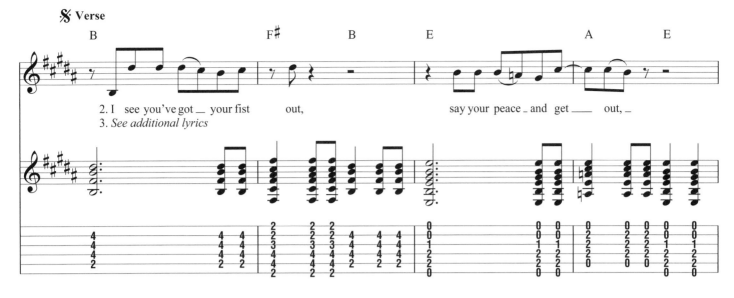

2. I see you've got __ your fist out, say your peace __ and get ____ out, __
3. *See additional lyrics*

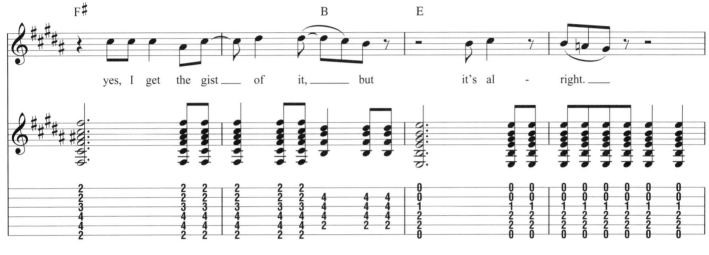

yes, I get the gist __ of it, _____ but it's al - right. ____

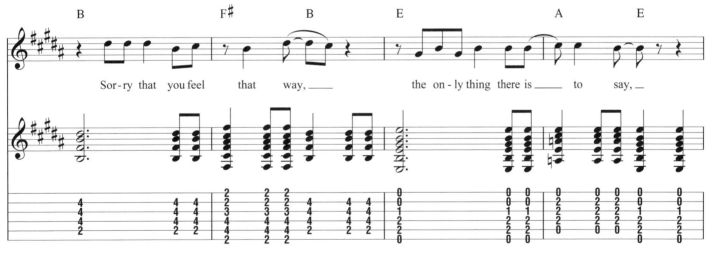

Sor-ry that you feel that way, ____ the on - ly thing there is ____ to say, _

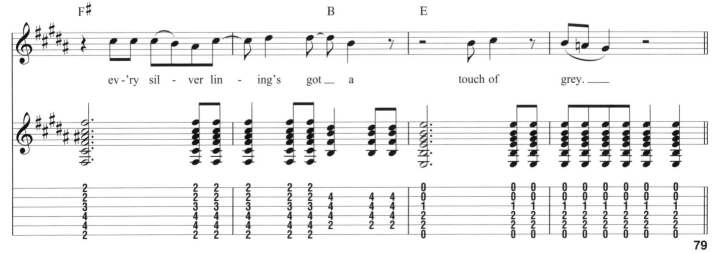

ev-'ry sil - ver lin - ing's got a touch of grey. ____

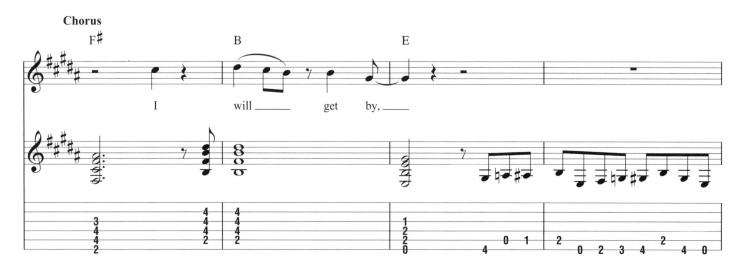

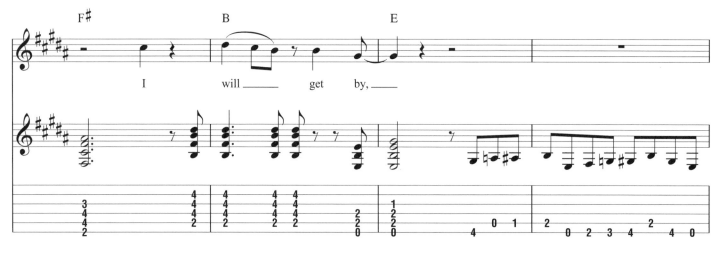

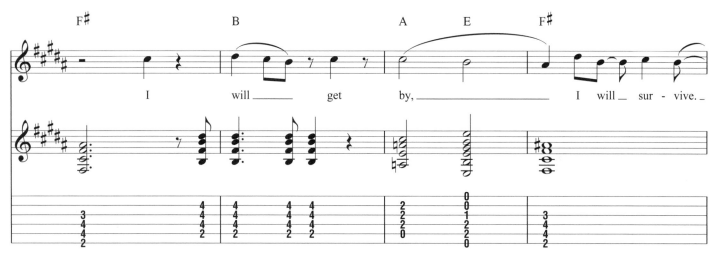

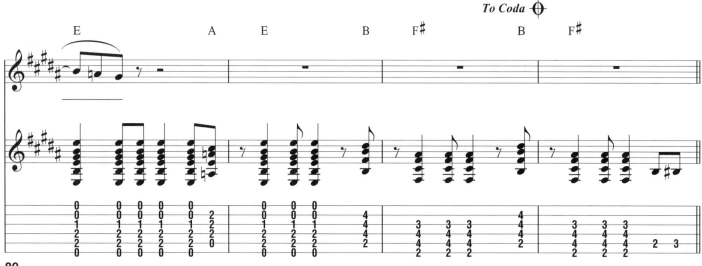

Bridge

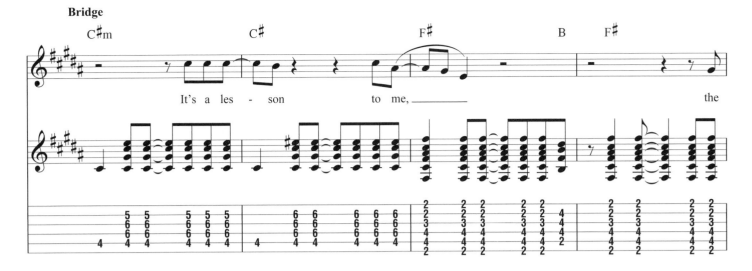

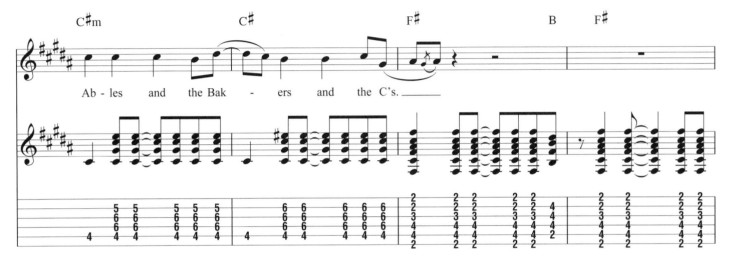

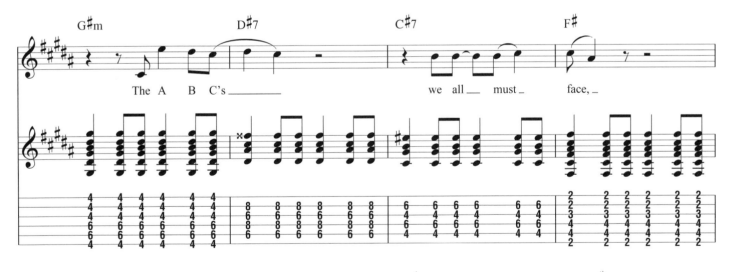

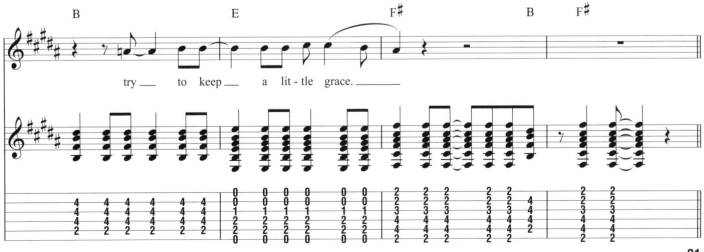

Guitar Solo

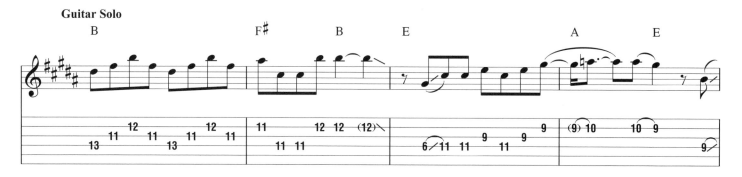

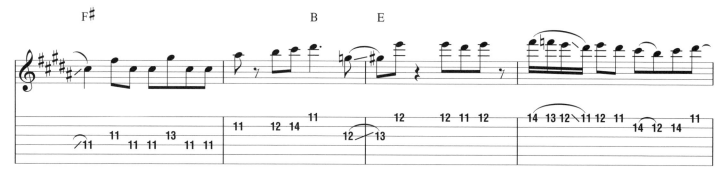

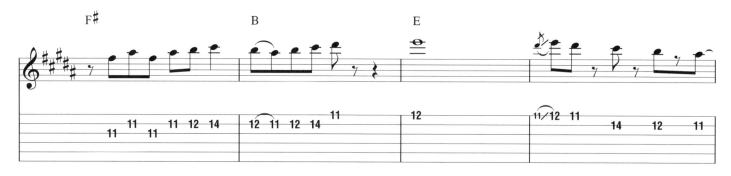

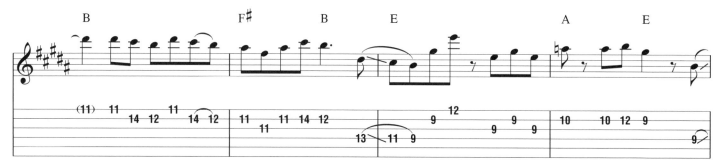

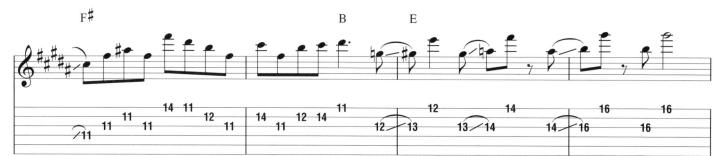

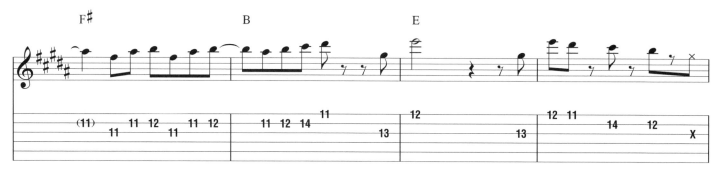

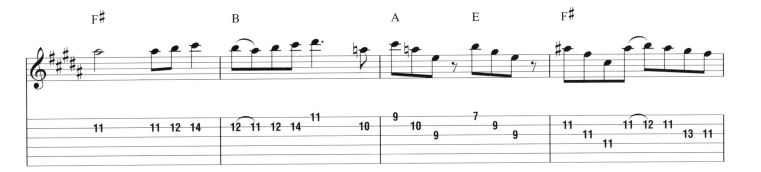

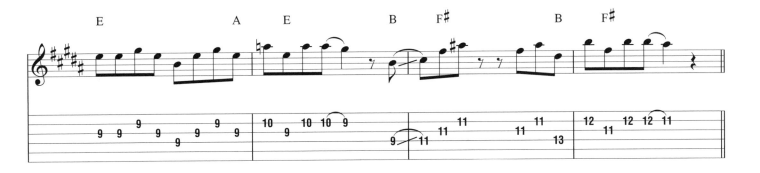

Bridge

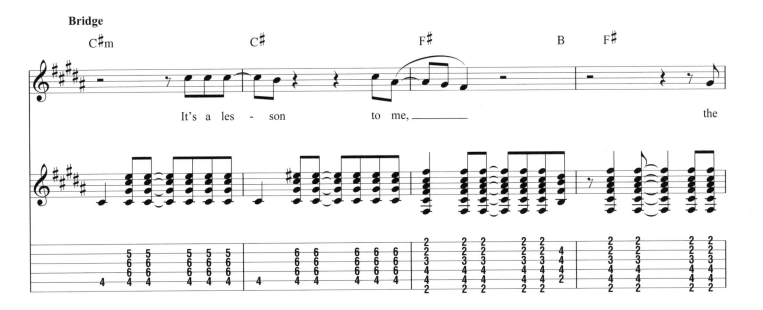

It's a les - son to me, _____ the

Del - tas and the East _____ and the freeze. _____

D.S. al Coda

 Coda

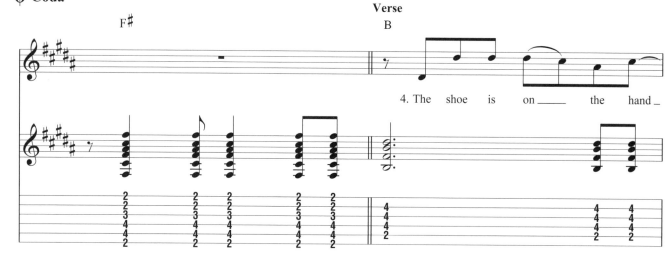

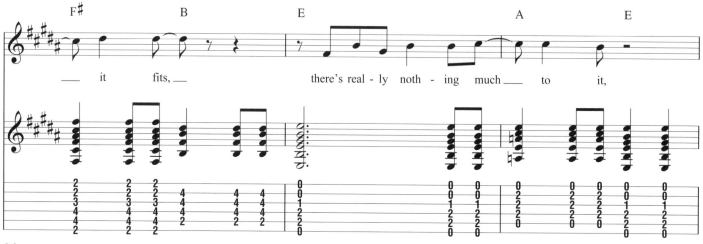

84

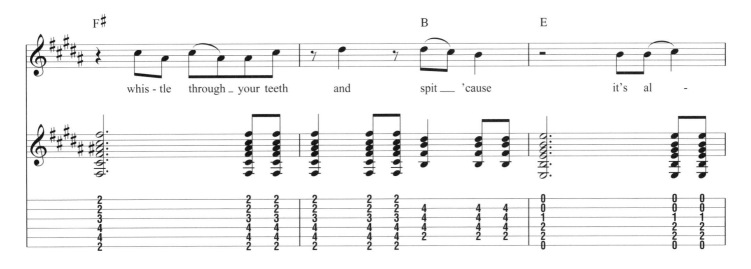

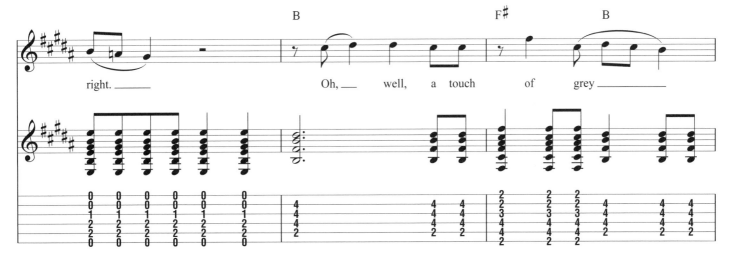

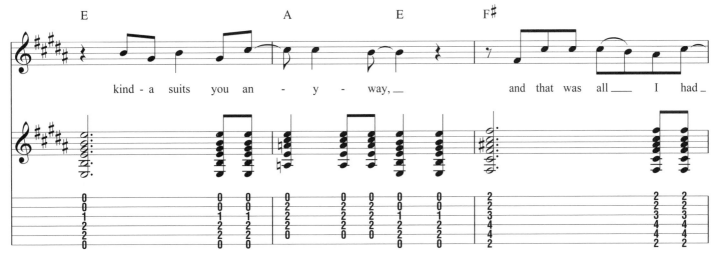

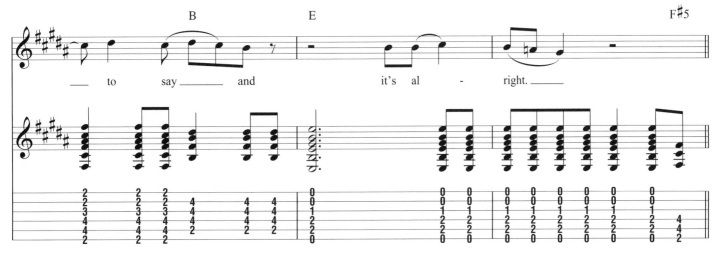

Chorus

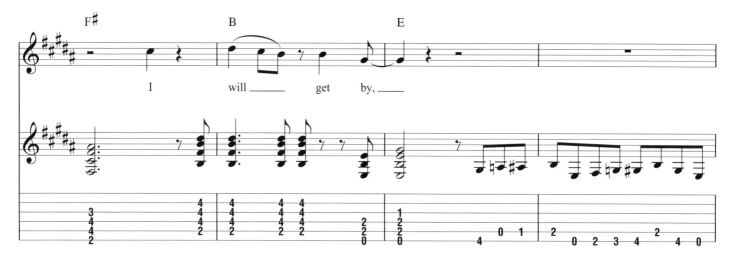

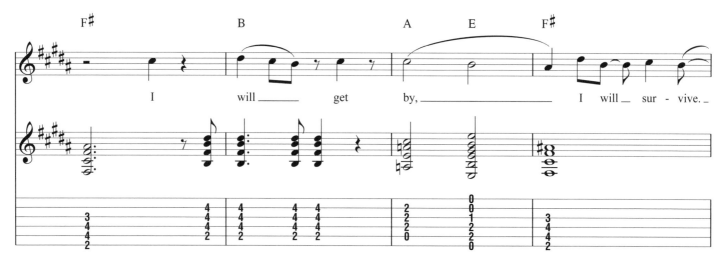

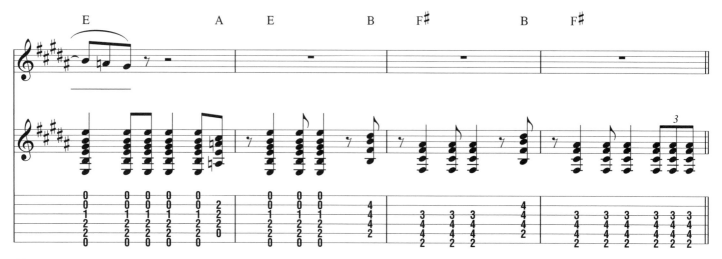

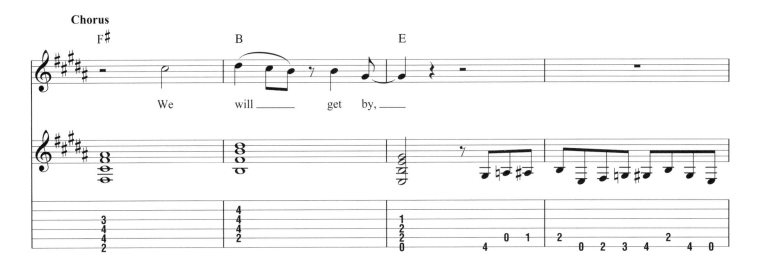

We will _____ get by, _____

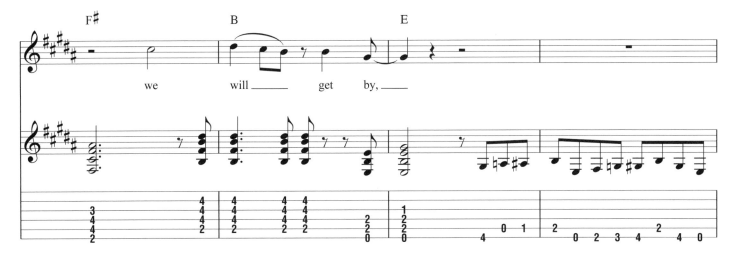

we will _____ get by, _____

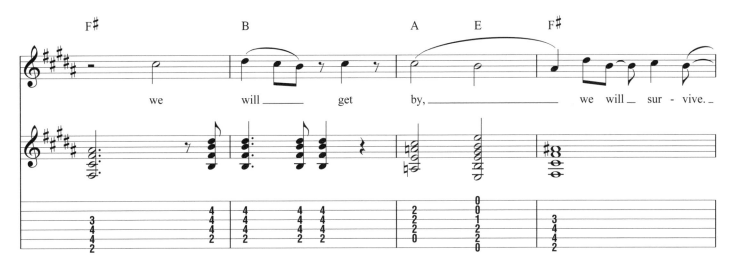

we will _____ get by, _____ we will __ sur - vive. __

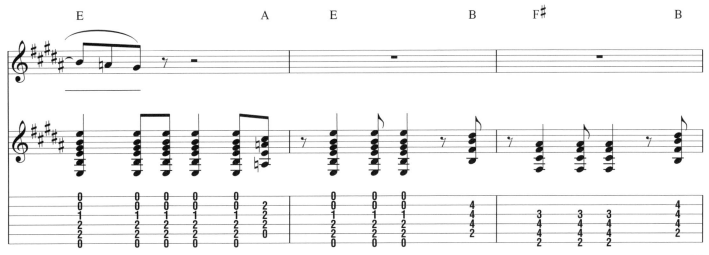

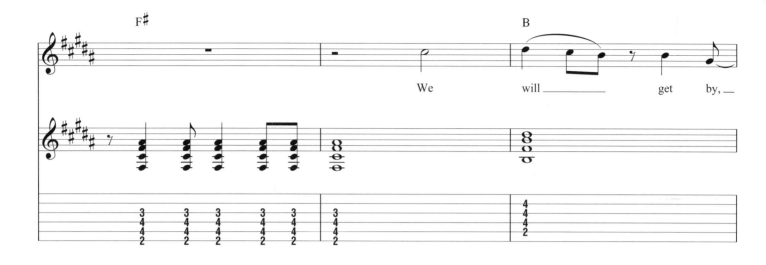

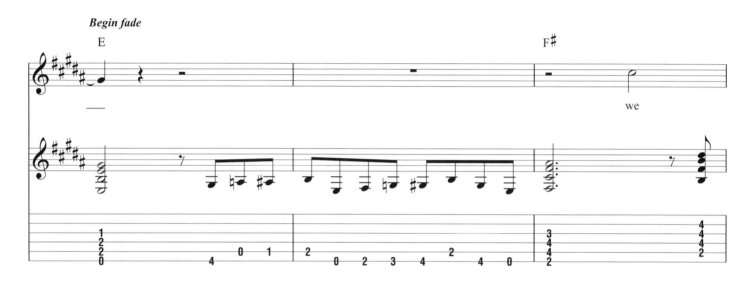

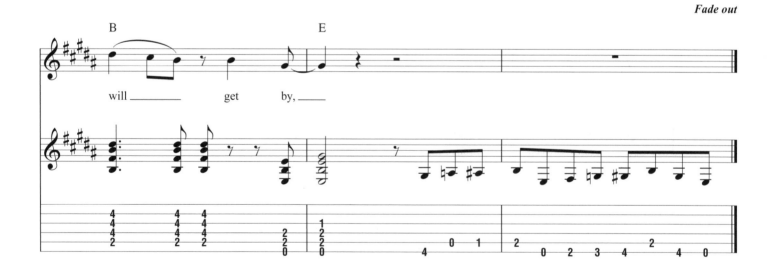

Additional Lyrics

3. I know the rent is in arrears,
   The dog has not been fed in years.
   It's even worse than it appears,
   But it's alright.
   Cows giving kerosene,
   Kid can't read at seventeen.
   The words he knows are all obscene,
   But it's alright.